ULTIMATE SURVIVAL
FOR KIDS

6 IN 1
ADVENTURE HANDBOOK

Welcome to the Ultimate Survival Skills for Kids, where adventure meets wisdom, and preparedness is your superpower!

Are you a kid who loves the idea of survival? Do you know how to thrive in any situation? Could we catapult you into the jungle, or drop you into a desert? Could you safely explore an isolated island, or be sent upstream to a waterfall?

Have you ever wondered what it takes to outsmart a wild creature or navigate through the depths of the forest like a true survival pro? Well, wonder no more because this book is your ticket to becoming the ultimate survival guru!

Now, you might be thinking, "Why do I need to know this stuff?" Trust me, I get it. Your days are filled with school, friends, and epic quests in video games. But let me tell you a secret: being prepared for emergencies is like having a secret weapon in your back pocket. Whether you're trekking through the jungle or just chilling in your backyard, knowing how to handle tricky situations can turn you from zero to hero in no time.

So, what exactly does this book have in store for you? Buckle up because we're diving headfirst into the wild and wonderful world of survival skills. From mastering the art of navigation using only the stars to building a cozy shelter fit for a king (or queen!), we've got everything you need to conquer the great outdoors like a champ.

But that's not all! Get ready for cool projects, brain-teasing puzzles, and quizzes that'll put your survival knowledge to the test. Plus, we'll sprinkle in some fascinating trivia to keep you on your toes.

And here's the cherry on top: as a special bonus, we've included a top-secret "Bonus Zombie Apocalypse Survival Guide" at the end of this book. Because let's face it, you never know when the undead might come knocking!

So, gear up, sharpen your wits, and get ready to face the ultimate challenge in survival.

CONTENTS

Section 1: Wilderness Survival...8

Fun Fact!...8

Navigating Wild Adventures:
Basic Techniques for Staying Safe 9

What is the wilderness?.. 10

Mastering Navigation with a
Compass and the Stars..14

Without the stars (or perhaps a more
straightforward method to find north
and south), is to use a compass..16

Wild Defender: A Fun Guide to Protecting
Yourself in Nature's Realm..19

Outsmarting Wild Creatures:
A Guide to Evading Animals 24

Shelter Crafting: Building Your Wild Haven..................27

Blaze Your Trail: A Wildfire Adventure
in Fire Lighting – How to Light a Fire................................ 29

Cool Project: Create Your Own Compass..........................31

Trivia #1 33

Wilderness Survival Word Search Puzzle....................... 36

Section 2: First Aid and Emergency Care 37

Fun Fact!...37

Basic First Aid Techniques: Be a First Aid
Hero, Even in Tough Situations! 39

Life-Saving Skills: How to Perform
CPR Like a Pro! 43

Signaling for Help: Catching the Eye of Rescue............ 48

Have you heard of Morse code?.. 49

Finding Safe Drinking Water:
Nature's Liquid Gold.. 53

Cool Project: Crafting Your First Aid Kit -
A DIY Adventure in Safety 56

Trivia #2 58

First Aid & Emergency Care Crossword Puzzle............ 61

Section 3: Street Smarts.. 63

Fun Fact!.. 63

How to Stay Safe in Tricky Situations! 65

Stay Safe by City Streets 70

Stay Safe in a Remote Village 73

Trivia #3 74

Street Smart Maze... 77

Section 4: Surviving Natural Disasters 78

Fun Fact!.. 78

Surviving a Hurricane: A Kid's Guide 80

Surviving a Tornado: A Kid's Guide 83

Surviving a Flood: What Kids Need to Know 86

How to Survive a Tsunami 90

How to Survive an Earthquake... 93

How to Avoid Being Struck by Lightning 97

Cool Craft: Make a Tornado in a Bottle!........................... 99

Trivia #4 101

Surviving Natural Disasters
Word Search Puzzle 104

Section 5: Human Hazards 105

Fun Fact! 105

How to Escape from a Burning Building 107

How to Survive Being Trapped
in a Car Going Underwater 110

Escaping the Elevator:
What to Do When You're Stuck 114

Caught in a Rip Tide: How to
Stay Safe in Strong Currents 117

Cool Craft: Create an Emergency Escape Plan 120

Trivia #5 122

Human Hazards Crossword Puzzle 125

Section 6: Animal Dangers 128

Fun Fact! 128

SSSSSnake Encounters 130

Bear Encounter Escape Guide:
Be Bear Aware! 133

Bee Encounter Escape Guide:
Buzzing Away Safely! 137

Spider Encounter Survival Guide:
Greeting Venomous Spiders! 141

Sting and Bite Guide: Heal the Hurt! 145

Bee Stings 146

Spider Bites 147

Mosquito Bites 148

Tick Bites 149

Cool Craft: Build a Bug House or Hotel..........................152

Trivia #6 154

Animal Dangers Maze 157

**Recap of Key Survival
Techniques Learned in 10!** 159

Here's the big question: are you ready? 161

**Bonus Section: How to Survive
a Zombie Apocalypse!**..164

Zombie Apocalypse Maze 167

Trivia Answers 168

Trivia #1: 168

Trivia #2: 168

Triva #3: 168

Trivia #4: 169

Trivia #5: 169

Trivia #6 170

First Aid & Emergency Care
Crossword Puzzle Answers..171

Human Hazards Crossword
Puzzle Answers 172

Wilderness Survival Word Search
Puzzle Answers 173

Surviving Natural Disasters
Word Search Puzzle Answers..174

Section 1

WILDERNESS SURVIVAL

Fun Fact!

Did you know that if you're lost in the wilderness, you can use the stars to find your way? In this chapter, you'll learn this amazing trick and many more cool survival skills that will turn you into a real-life adventurer! Get ready to discover the secrets of the wild and how to stay safe while exploring nature's wonders.

Navigating Wild Adventures: Basic Techniques for Staying Safe

Right now, you are clutching the ultimate survival guide in your hands! Treat this as your treasure trove of awesome tips to help you thrive, survive, and succeed in any adventurous situation.

Once you're done, you'll have the skillset and knowledge that any kid needs to know for wilderness survival!

What is the Wilderness?

The wilderness refers to any place or location that's off-grid, untamed, or … just wild (it's called the wilderness, after all!). Since the beginning of time, there have been humans hoping to find and explore the most remote places on Earth. Are you one of them?

Explorers want to embrace exciting, natural landscapes. Human contact might be minimal. In fact, you might not see another human at all in these types of places… But these places offer raw beauty, awesome landscapes, and adventurous terrains! Not only that, but you might be more likely to see wonderful wildlife.

From thick jungles where tigers roam, to icy landscapes inhabited by polar bears, and distant shores where flamingos flap, each habitat offers the opportunity to observe and appreciate the amazing diversity of life on Earth.

Some people like to experience conservation efforts when they travel. This means that they hope to care for, or even participate in projects for preserving endangered species and their habitats. Would you be interested in traveling to support conservation efforts?

You'll certainly need to learn more about animal safety in the wild. In fact, whatever you end up doing in the wilderness, knowing how to be safe is crucial! You'll only survive by staying safe.

So, to navigate your wild adventures, start here with some general basic techniques for staying safe.

Firstly, tell someone where you're headed. It's no use wandering off into the wilderness with nobody knowing you're there. You've got a plan for where you want to go, right? (It's even better for safety if you can buddy up and go on adventures with a friend.)

Secondly, make sure you've got a backpack of essentials. You can't survive without hydration, so a drink is a must! Food and snacks will also be vital, even if you plan on finding some nibbles along the way. Knowing how to identify plants and berries you can eat might also be a good idea (there are many that you can't eat – so check that out, too!)

Thirdly, think about shelter. You'll need somewhere to protect yourself from storms, burning sunshine, and danger. Plus, you'll need somewhere to rest your head and sleep. Keeping a tarp or small tent inside your backpack is a top safety tip for surviving the adventure. Later in this book, you'll learn how to craft a shelter using nature.

Lastly, plan for an emergency. What's your backup plan going to be if things go wrong? Will you have any phone signal, or where's the nearest village or town to find help?

Delve into the rest of our awesome guide to truly get to grips with navigating the wilderness, and you'll be ready in no time for a truly amazing adventure!

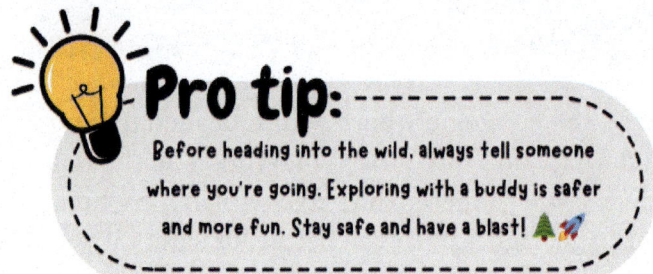

Pro tip:
Before heading into the wild, always tell someone where you're going. Exploring with a buddy is safer and more fun. Stay safe and have a blast! 🌲🚀

Mastering Navigation with a Compass and the Stars

After packing your essentials, you'll take your first steps to start your adventure. Even if you're hoping to explore and go with the flow, you'll still need some sort of plan for where you're headed, whether it's following a track or aiming for a particular destination.

Therefore, make sure you master basic navigation. Not only is this useful for direction, but it's even more useful to know how to navigate if you get lost! No explorer wants to end up completely lost, as this can be very dangerous.

Did you know that sailors used to navigate by using the stars? And explorers once used the stars to find their way through forests and jungles. Before Global Positioning Systems (GPS – a Satnav is one) there wasn't technology to help with navigation, so people had to rely on nature instead.

Experts could use the stars a bit like a treasure map. Each star has its own place in the sky, but lots of explorers use a big star called Polaris. Some people refer to Polaris as the North Star, and if you can find it, then you know which way North is. Anyone can learn to find Polaris. Learning the rest of the stars to help guide your journey requires you to scrub up on some extra knowledge, though!

The best time to spot Polaris is when the sky is clear and dark. Locate the Big Dipper first (this is a group of seven stars that form a shape like a saucepan. It's one of the brightest star patterns to look for). Imagine a line running through the two outer stars of the Big Dipper's 'saucepan' and imagine repeating this line about five times. Along this long line (probably more towards the end of it) you should be able to spot Polaris! The star should look still (other stars might look like they're moving). It should be a little brighter compared to the other stars by it.

If you can find Polaris, you'll know you're facing north. You'll face south if you do a 180-degree turn away from Polaris.

Without the stars (or perhaps a more straightforward method to find north and south), is to use a compass.

To master navigation in the wilderness, you should certainly master this pocket-sized tool. A compass is a gizmo that helps you to find your way. Compasses point out which way is North, South, East, and West. A compass works using magnetic force; it has a needle in the middle that will be drawn towards the magnetic North Pole.

On your compass, you'll need to see where the symbols are for N (North), E (East), S (South), and W (West). You'll also need to find the direction-of-travel arrow.

On your compass, the direction-of-travel arrow points in the direction you want to go. Make sure you hold your compass flat and steady in front of you (and keep it away from metal objects to avoid any magnetic interference!). While holding the compass, turn your body until the needle lines up with the North symbol on the compass dial… then stop! Now you'll know which way North is.

Mastering the use of a compass can be a bit fiddly at first, so be patient, and keep trying. Before your trip, practice using your compass in familiar surroundings, where you can check if you're using it correctly. It might be a good idea to rope in an adult, or use your compass with a map in hand, to check you've got the hang of it!

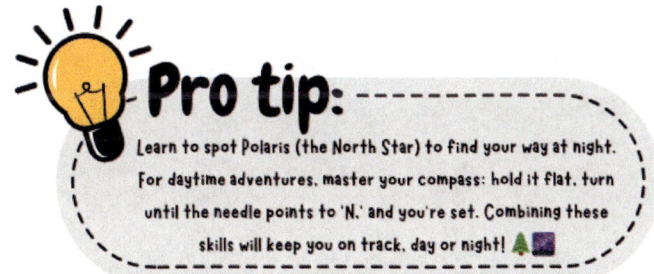

Pro tip: Learn to spot Polaris (the North Star) to find your way at night. For daytime adventures, master your compass: hold it flat, turn until the needle points to 'N,' and you're set. Combining these skills will keep you on track, day or night! 🌲🗺️

Wild Defender: A Fun Guide to Protecting Yourself in Nature's Realm

Even if you're studying your compass as you start your journey, keep your wits about you... You won't get very far if you don't spot the avalanche heading towards you, or the volcano erupting at your side.

Look up! Look around! Use your senses to protect yourself as you step into nature's realm.

Know your environment. If you're starting on tough terrain, keep looking ahead for unsteady patches or difficult climbs. Is there a cliff or canyon ahead? How will you cross this? If you're starting by a swift river, what will you be able to grab onto if you fall in?

Make sure you are dressed for success! High heels in the forest? Absolutely not! You'll need sturdy shoes that can help you tackle anything, and lightweight layers of clothing to adapt to changing weather conditions. A sun hat and sun cream should never go amiss either. Don't get burnt as you'll only regret your lobster-look later (and it will feel super sore under the straps of your backpack!)

With your skin protected, make sure you are using your sense of touch to help you in other ways. Test how steady a rock is by placing your foot on it first to see if it wobbles (if it wobbles, try a different route).

If there's a tangle of overgrowth ahead, use a stick to decide whether you'll be able to make it through or not. Ideally, however, you want to leave nature as 'untouched' as possible, so perhaps go a different way if your route will involve you bashing down roots and leaves. Go find a clearer pathway.

Try to leave no trace, where you can. This includes packing away any litter and checking that you haven't left any belongings behind. While you won't find a bin around you or anybody telling you off for dropping rubbish, this doesn't offer any excuse for doing so. In fact, it could be very harmful to wildlife and plants, so take everything with you.

Don't forget your sense of hearing as well. Be prepared to listen and listen well! To truly protect yourself in nature, listen out for any unusual sounds or noises. The sounds might be worth enjoying (like a beautiful songbird or a sign of civilization), or it could be a warning of something to be aware of. Either way, trust your instincts. Make sure what you can hear makes you feel safe.

When it comes to protecting yourself further, you should also use your sense of smell. Does it smell like something is burning? Can you see smoke and a big fire ahead? Use your phone to alert the closest emergency services and walk away to safety. Does it seem like the smell of burning could be another traveler enjoying a campfire? If so, perhaps check it out and speak to the person. There should also be somebody monitoring a fire. If there's not, it's a danger to all life and 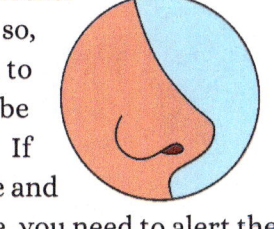 potentially a wildfire. In this case, you need to alert the fire brigade quickly, as fire spreads very quickly – especially where there are trees or materials nearby. Get as far away as you can in this scenario.

Other things you might be able to smell in the wilderness include fresh pines, wildflowers, or herbs and plants. These smells might be inviting and invigorating. Some aromatic plants even release oils into the air that offer a calming experience and smell amazing! In this scenario, it might be a lovely place to stop off and embrace the outdoor experience.

Be mindful of your sense of taste, however. You can't go picking things up and eating them (however good they look) without checking that they are safe first. To protect yourself, having a small guidebook in your bag is a wise idea, as then you can refer to information and pictures to be sure of whether you can eat a plant you've found.

You'll have the most fun in your environment if you've taken sensible steps to protect yourself. Use all senses to do so, and your adventure will continue in the best way possible!

Pro tip: Use all your senses to stay aware of your surroundings. Keep an eye out for potential hazards like avalanches or steep cliffs, and listen for unusual sounds that might indicate danger. Staying alert keeps you safe and ready for anything!

Outsmarting Wild Creatures: A Guide to Evading Animals

Like you'll be using your senses to navigate your surroundings, you won't be the only living thing using your senses.

In our guide, we've already touched on being able to see amazing animals, but you'll only survive the experience if you know how to encounter wild creatures effectively!

You need to know how to outsmart wild creatures: remember to stay one step ahead.

In the thick forests, you should prepare to encounter big creatures like the grizzly bear, or wild dogs and cougars sniffing around in the underbrush. If you're in the open plains, you'll come across grazing animals like gazelles or the bison. Whilst these animals are shy creatures, they are often being watched by hunting predators like coyotes, cheetahs, lions or wolves (depending on where you are!).

Birds of prey like eagles or hawks may be looking down from above, hoping to swoop down for a tasty treat! And if you're by water, you should keep a look out for crocodiles or alligators, and if you're in the ocean, know how to spot a stingray, shark, or tingling jellyfish!

So how are you going to do this?

You're going to need to respect their space! Wild animals are usually fearful of humans... and if they're not fearful, they could be curious, so give the creature plenty of space to behave as naturally as possible. Find a perfect spot to stay still and watch carefully. Stay alert in case the animal's behaviour changes.

You might want to make some noise as you approach your observing spot. Gently clapping, humming, or talking quietly lets animals know that someone is approaching. This gives them a chance to move away before you get too close, and it also gives them a chance to be aware of another presence.

If the animal chooses to hide away, don't follow them in case they feel threatened. Leave them be.

If you feel disappointed, try different tactics to spot awesome animals. You can follow paw tracks or footprints, look out for droppings (poop), or spy scratches on trees. These will signal that animals are nearby, and if you wait patiently, one might turn up! If you're lucky, a group might appear together.

Like humans, animals feel better protected in groups. If you're traveling with others, make sure to stick together when looking for wildlife.

Have some safety gear just in case things take a turn for the worse. If an animal starts to look aggressive, prepare to act. Depending on the animal, this might mean slowly walking away, or it might mean you need to resort to something like pepper spray if the animal starts to approach you in a hostile way.

Make sure you know when to back off. You'll avoid an animal becoming agitated or aggressive if you pick up the sense that something might go wrong. Move away, and never attempt to touch a wild animal – even if it seems friendly.

Only watch.

Pro tip: When encountering wild animals, always give them plenty of space. Make some noise to let them know you're coming, and never follow them if they hide. Observe from a distance and stay alert to their behavior. 🌲 ..

Shelter Crafting: Building Your Wild Haven

After a busy day out on foot, you'll need time for your body to rest, recuperate and sleep. You'll never survive your journey without adequate sleep, which helps your body to refuel and repair itself.

Whilst you might have a tent, tarp, or sleeping bag in your pack ready for this, you could also craft your own shelter.

Who doesn't love a bit of den building?

To build your wild haven, find an open spot. Make sure it's also an area where there are plenty of fallen branches and leaves available to you – and perhaps any other suitable materials you can find – to construct your shelter with.

Collect your materials. Sturdy branches will be best for building your den with. If a branch easily snaps, it's probably rotten and might break in the night or bring your shelter to collapse, so make sure your sticks are strong!

Gather up moss or leaves that can be used to insulate and cover your den.

Once you've got everything you'll need,

assess your materials. Start thinking about how you will construct the frame. It might help to lay it out on the floor first, so you can adjust before trying to put it all up.

When you're ready, leave the branches against each other to build a structure. Did you know that triangle shapes tend to be the strongest? Aim for a triangle shape if you can. But don't forget to leave yourself an entrance!

Fill in the walls of your structure with twigs and smaller branches. You can weave them together to make your shelter even more sturdy. Then add leaves, moss, or grass to the outer 'walls' of your den, because this will help retain some warmth and protect you a little more from external elements.

Blaze Your Trail: A Wildfire Adventure in Fire Lighting – How to Light a Fire

Most explorers want a campfire once they've set up a shelter. As I'm sure you wise folks already know, fire can be dangerous, so make sure you know what you're doing around fire.

Pick a good spot to build your fire. Somewhere that is dry and clear is best: make sure nothing around will catch fire.

Next, prepare your fire by gathering sticks of different sizes. Smaller twigs can be useful as kindling (kindling refers to things that set light quickly). Dry leaves make good kindling, too.

If possible, use rocks to form a circle around where you are going to make the fire, because this will help contain your fire inside an awesome pit!

Pop the kindling in the middle of your fire pit, and then place sticks across the middle in a crisscross manner. Place some larger sticks or logs over the top like a teepee, but take care not to use too many, or they'll fall, and put your small fire out! Also, fire needs some air flow to get going.

Hopefully you've prepared for this moment, and you have matches or a lighter in your backpack. If you don't, brace yourself to make a fire from scratch! You can make fire in a few different ways (but don't try this at home!)

Friction-based: you might have seen people doing this on films and TV – it looks easier than it is! Rubbing a hard stick against a softer piece of wood creates friction. If you create an ember (small flame) transfer it to your kindling. Make sure you are close to your kindling at the start, though! This technique certainly takes patience.

Magnifying glass: should you happen to be carrying a magnifying glass (which you might to spot bugs and beasties), then you can use it to start your fire. You'll need sunlight (this method will fail in the rain). Hold the magnifying glass at an angle, and with lots of patience and luck, your kindling might start to smolder and catch alight.

Cool Project: Create Your Own Compass

It seems we have the basics covered for your initiation into your wilderness survival!

Before we get down to more of the nitty-gritty, you might like to get creative.

Earlier you read about compasses, but did you know that you can create your own compass? Let us tell you how!

You'll need an adult to be willing to source a few materials for you. These include:

1. Sewing needle or a pin (these can be rather 'ouchy', so get an adult!)
2. Magnet (you can use a small bar from the back of a fridge magnet)
3. Cork, leaf, or a little bit of Styrofoam (you might have some of this from parcel packaging)
4. Small bowl of water (enough water for the Styrofoam to float in)
5. Optional paper clip

To start creating your compass, you need the needle or pin to become magnetic. Rub the needle or pin along the magnet (keeping to one direction) many times. This will magnetize it if you do it enough times.

Next, place the magnetized pin or needle onto the cork, leaf, or piece of Styrofoam.

Carefully place into the bowl of water, making sure it can float.

Watch carefully. Wait for the needle to come to rest.

If all works well, the needle should line up with the magnetic field of the Earth, and roughly point towards the North.

Keep in mind that your compass is homemade and don't be too disappointed if it doesn't work out the first time… or the second time… you can always try again.

This activity is a great way to explore electric fields and magnetism.

Have fun experimenting!

Trivia #1

1. What is the wilderness?

   A. The wilderness refers to a hot, sunny holiday at a hotel.
   B. The wilderness refers to any place or location that's off-grid, untamed or … just wild.
   C. The wilderness refers to a beach that is clean and maintained.
   D. The wilderness refers to wild beasts chasing people!

2. What does it mean by 'conservation efforts?'

   A. This means that people hope to care for, or even participate in projects for preserving endangered species and their habitats.
   B. This means that animals hope to care for preserving endangered species and habitats.
   C. This means having an extra bag to travel with.
   D. This means enjoying and participating in projects to rescue missing people.

3. What do we mean by 'shelter'?

    A. building a big fire
    B. creating a statue
    C. somewhere to protect yourself from storms, burning sunshine, and danger
    D. somewhere to hide your stolen property

4. How did sailors use to navigate?

    A. by using trees
    B. by asking mermaids
    C. by using the stars
    D. by using the ocean floor

5. What is the nickname for the star called 'Polaris'?

    A. North Star
    B. East Star
    C. South Star
    D. West Star

6. What is the purpose of using a compass in the wilderness?

    A) To make friends with animals
    B) To spot hidden treasure
    C) To navigate and find directions
    D) To make fire

7. How can you protect yourself from the sun while exploring nature?

    A) Wear high heels
    B) Wear a sun hat and sunscreen
    C) Wear shorts and a tank top

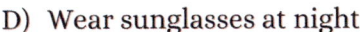

    D) Wear sunglasses at night

8. What should you do if you smell smoke and see a big fire ahead?

    A) Take a nap
    B) Walk towards the fire to investigate
    C) Use your phone to alert emergency services and walk away to safety
    D) Ignore it and continue your journey

9. What is the purpose of making noise as you approach animals in the wilderness?

    A) To scare them away
    B) To make them curious
    C) To let them know you're approaching
    D) To make them attack you

10. What should you do if an animal becomes aggressive while you're in the wilderness?

    A) Approach it slowly
    B) Offer it food
    C) Try to pet it
    D) Prepare to act, depending on the animal, such as slowly walking away or using pepper spray

Wilderness Survival Word Search Puzzle

Welcome to the Wilderness Survival Word Search Puzzle! Can you find all the hidden words related to wilderness survival? Test your skills and see how many you can discover!

ADVENTURE
ANIMAL
COMPASS
CONSERVATION

EMERGENCY
EXPLORATION
FIRE
NAVIGATION

SAFETY
SHELTER
STARS
SURVIVAL

TERRAIN
WILDERNESS
WILDLIFE

Section 2

FIRST AID AND EMERGENCY CARE

Fun Fact!

Did you know that you can be a first aid hero even in tough situations? In this section, you'll learn how to handle cuts, scrapes, burns, and even perform lifesaving CPR! Discover the essential first-aid techniques that will turn you into a rescue hero and ensure you're always prepared for any adventure. Get ready to save the day and learn the skills that could make you a real-life lifesaver!

Basic First Aid Techniques: Be a First Aid Hero, Even in Tough Situations!

Are you prepared for someone getting hurt? Let's face it, big adventures come with risk. Risk can be fun, but risk can also lead to accidents. Let's figure out some basic first-aid techniques to turn you into a rescue hero!

What do we mean by first aid? Well, it's the task of helping someone sick or injured until doctors or paramedics can take over. And the great thing is that anyone – of any age – can learn simple first-aid techniques.

We will start with how to treat cuts and scrapes. As a kid, this is a common occurrence, right? If someone gets a scrape, the first thing you should do is clean it with soap and water. Pop a band-aid or a bandage on the wound to keep it clean and help it heal faster. Simple, huh?

But what if someone gets bumped on the head? Head injuries can be serious, so you should tell them to sit or lie down. Put something cold on the bump, like an ice pack or a bag of frozen vegetables wrapped in a cloth or towel. (The ice will stick to the person's skin if you don't cover it with material. While this isn't a huge problem, ice to the skin is *pretty* uncomfortable…)

And if someone gets a nosebleed? Don't panic! It might look much worse than it is! Have the person sit up straight and lean forward slightly. Grab a container or tissue to catch the blood in. If the nose continues to bleed, some people recommend pinching the person's nose with your fingers, just below the bony part, and holding it for about 10 minutes.

On your grand adventure, there is a risk of burns, whether from a campfire or sliding down something and receiving a friction burn. If this happens to someone, cool the burn with cold water for at least 10 minutes. Afterward, cover the burn with a clean, dry cloth or bandage (dig into your trusty first-aid kit!). And whatever you do, leave the blisters alone! Blisters form as part of the healing process, so you need to leave them be.

And finally, a big thing to deal with is choking. Would you know what to do?

If someone chokes, encourage them to cough as hard as they can. If they can't cough it out, give them five back blows between the shoulder blades and five abdominal thrusts (this is also known as the Heimlich Manoeuvre).

If possible, ask someone nearby to call the emergency services while you are doing this, as then you can seek further advice, and someone will soon be on their way to help you. You will need to keep repeating the back blows and abdominal thrusts until the object comes out, or help arrives.

And stay calm! Even if you don't feel it, you want the other person to feel as reassured as possible.

If you can remain calm in a tricky situation, it will help you on your way to being a hero and potentially saving a life!

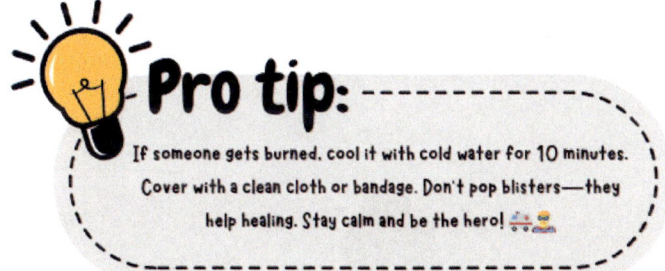

Pro tip:
If someone gets burned, cool it with cold water for 10 minutes. Cover with a clean cloth or bandage. Don't pop blisters—they help healing. Stay calm and be the hero! 🚑🦸

Life-Saving Skills: How to Perform CPR Like a Pro!

Following first aid, giving CPR is a life-saving skill. In this section, let's check out how to perform CPR like a pro!

CPR stands for Cardiopulmonary Resuscitation. Cardio refers to the heart, and pulmonary refers to the lungs. Resuscitation means to revive or recover. CPR is a super skill that can save someone's life if they're not breathing, or their heart has stopped beating.

Ideally, you'll attend a real-life training course to best know how to administer this. However, any awareness you can have (or online videos you could watch) could be vital in knowing how to help somebody out.

For now, reading our step-by-step CPR will springboard your basic knowledge:

1. Assess the scene for your safety:

Make sure the area is safe for the person, and safe for you to look for help. Watch out for fires, traffic, or anything else that might worry you. If it's safe, then you'll be able to go ahead and approach the person who needs help!

2. See if the person responds:

Tap the person on the shoulder, and ask "Are you okay?" If you get no response, it's time to start CPR!

3. Call for help:

If there's someone else nearby, get them to call the emergency services. You'll want to call for the emergency services as soon as you can. Make the call yourself if nobody else is around. (Top tip: you'll be able to receive instructions for delivering CPR when you phone the emergency services!)

4. Chest compressions:

Place the back of your hand (the 'heel' of your hand') on the middle of the person's chest. Place your other hand on top and interlock your fingers. Next, you need to learn over the person - keeping your arms straight - and push down hard and fast. It's a bit like you are pumping up the heart. For CPR, you aim for around 100-120 compressions per minute, but many suggest remembering a song to get the compression 'beat.' Lots of people use the chorus of a famous old song:

'Nellie the Elephant packed her trunk

And said goodbye to the circus

Off she went with a trumpety-trump

Trump, trump, trump

Nellie the Elephant packed her trunk

And trundled back to the jungle

Off she went with a trumpety-trump

Trump, trump, trump…'

('Nellie the Elephant' was originally written by Ralph Butler and Peter Hart in 1956. It was first recorded by singer Mandy Miller).

Don't worry if you don't know this song: search online for 'CPR song lists' and use a respected source to advise you of a different song!

5. Time for rescue breaths:
   After every 30 chest compressions (that's each time you push down), it's time for rescue breaths. You need to tilt the person's head back slightly (lift their chin gently with your hand). Before giving the breath, pinch the person's nose shut and put your mouth over theirs. Now give two breaths into their mouth, with each breath lasting around one second. Wait to see if their chest starts to rise.

6. After the rescue breaths, return to chest compressions. If you've got someone else around, you can switch if you get tired. Keep this going until the emergency team arrives! Remember: this is serious stuff! This process is designed to save a life. You could be a real-life hero. Take a CPR course if you want to rehearse and refine your survival skillset.

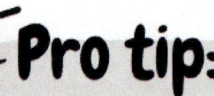

Pro tip:

When performing CPR, keep the beat with a familiar song like "Nellie the Elephant" to maintain the right rhythm of 100-120 chest compressions per minute. This helps you stay on track and could save a life! 🚑🧑‍⚕️

Signaling for Help: Catching the Eye of Rescue

Now, let's imagine you're on your big adventure when something goes wrong! You seriously need help. As you look around you, there's not a soul in your eyeline. You're alone! Instead of panicking, remember the following tips that tell you how to signal for help.

Catching the eye of a rescuer, or gathering attention in an emergency, can be crucial for surviving situations.

To do this effectively, you need to make yourself known!

If possible, make lots of noise! Start to shout – loudly and continually. Carrying a whistle in your backpack is a great idea to attract attention and will save you from needing to shout.

Also, the sound of a whistle carries further than your voice will. It is known that three short blasts of a whistle are a sign of distress, so if someone hears this, they should know that you need help!

If it's appropriate, you might also consider creating something visual for potential rescuers to see. Can you wave a flag? Can you use a mirror to create a flashing reflection using light? Have you got any colored clothing to wave?

If you're lost for a long time in a remote place, you could use rocks to spell out 'HELP' or 'SOS' that somebody might see if they fly over the area. If you spot a potential rescuer nearby, wave and attract attention as best as you can – make your distress visible. Put yourself in a position where you're likely to be seen, so be out in an open area where you can be spotted.

Have you heard of Morse code?

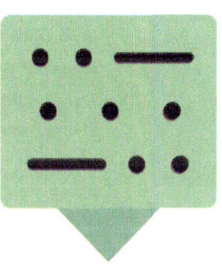

Every great explorer knows the basics of Morse code, as it's a signaling system used internationally. This means that it is a method of communication that remains the same across the globe.

Morse code is shown through short sounds (dots) and long sounds (dashes).

Here's the international representation of Morse code to check out:

A: .-

B: -...

C: -.-.

D: -..

E: .

F: ..-.

G: --.

H: ....

I: ..

J: .---

K: -.-

L: .-..

M: --

N: -.

O: ---

P: .--.

Q: --.-

R: .-.

S: ...

T: -

U: ..-

V: ...-

W: .--

X: -..-

Y: -.--

Z: --..

Using this, can you figure out SOS? (Maybe you've heard of SOS from TV or movies... the letters don't

50

stand for anything more than an easy pattern to remember!)

A dot, dot, dot is the letter 'S,' and a dash, dash, dash is the letter 'O.' Before phones, computers or devices existed, people used Morse code sometimes to get messages across visible distances.

Morse code can be really fun to learn, especially with friends. It's a great way to have a secret language amongst yourselves, either by using flashlights or tapping your fingers to represent the dots and dashes.

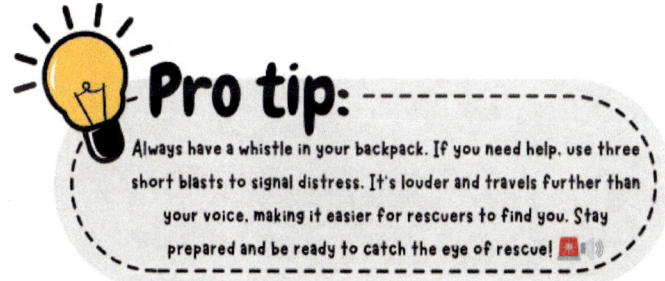

Pro tip: Always have a whistle in your backpack. If you need help, use three short blasts to signal distress. It's louder and travels further than your voice, making it easier for rescuers to find you. Stay prepared and be ready to catch the eye of rescue!

Finding Safe Drinking Water: Nature's Liquid Gold

Imagine exploring the wild and seeing the trees, the birds, and the rivers. Imagine trekking and getting completely lost in your adventure, when you suddenly realize how thirsty you are! On pulling out your drink bottle, you see that it's empty… you forgot to refill it when you were last in a village or a town. What are you going to do? How are you going to find safe water to drink?

Let's find out:

Look around for clear, flowing water. Avoid water that looks dirty or muddy – your eyes should tell you it's no good for drinking! Avoid stagnant water as well. Stagnant water is water that is still. This means it could have been there for too long and could also make you sick. Instead, look for clear, flowing water. Ideally, you want to look for a stream with water you can see through.

On collecting water, it is even better if you can filter it. This way, you can be sure that you're removing tiny particles and germs that might make you fall unwell. Having a water filtering system in your bag is a good top tip for traveling. You can also buy water 'filtering' tablets that you can pop into stream water, and it'll purify the water ready to drink.

If you don't have water filtering methods within your equipment, then there's another way to get clean water. Find a big, leafy green plant and tie a plastic bag tightly around a leafy branch. Wait a few hours, and water droplets will collect inside the bag. This process is called 'transpiration'. It is a method you can use to 'collect' clean water.

Fun thought! Water transpiration is a bit like plants 'sweating'. As the plants drink water from the soil through their roots, droplets then evaporate from the leaves through tiny holes.

Another top tip is to source dew in the morning. Dew is droplets of water that form on grass and leaves overnight. Using a towel or piece of clean material, collect as much dew as you can then wring it out into a pot or pan, and clean water awaits!

Finally, never drink water from puddles or unknown sources. Always ask an adult if you're unsure about the water's safety.

Use this know-how to stay hydrated and healthy on all your awesome explorations.

Cheers to Nature's liquid gold (water)!

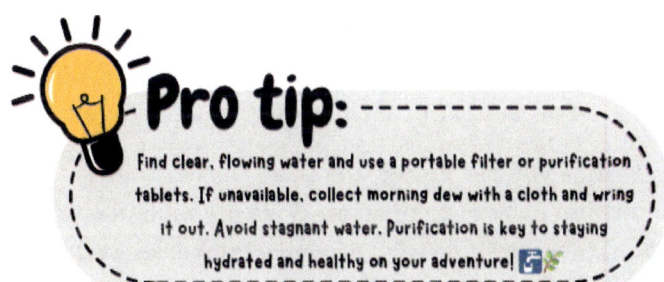

Pro tip: Find clear, flowing water and use a portable filter or purification tablets. If unavailable, collect morning dew with a cloth and wring it out. Avoid stagnant water. Purification is key to staying hydrated and healthy on your adventure!

Cool Project: Crafting Your First Aid Kit - A DIY Adventure in Safety

Using different items, you can make your own First Aid Kit. Consider this a DIY (Do It Yourself) approach to putting a kit together:

First up, you're going to need a container. Find something easy to take around with you: a plastic tub or a metal container with a secure lid works well.

Inside your kit, you'll need basic supplies:

- Adhesive bandages and plasters
- Sterile gauze pads
- Sterile saline solution for cleaning wounds (you can buy small-sized bottles to fit in a first aid kit)
- Disposable gloves
- Adhesive tape
- Antiseptic solution or wipes
- Small scissors
- Tweezers
- Safety pins

You'll also likely want to have some basic medications (but an adult must be involved for this part! Don't go finding any medications yourself. An adult is responsible for medication):

- Pain relief medication
- Antihistamine to address an allergic reaction
- Hydrocortisone cream to ease itching and rashes
- Anti-diarrhoea medication

Also, if you know that you and your family need a specific medication or they need an inhaler or an epi-pen, having an extra inside your first aid kit is a good idea!

Other things you might like to include for an adventurous trip might be insect repellent, sunscreen, and blister packs – there's nothing more annoying than getting a blister on a fun, wild trek.

Once you're satisfied you have the items you need, pop them into your container to create your own first aid kit! You might like to personalize the outside of your container with stickers. Inside, you might like to use Ziplock bags or smaller containers to organize everything.

Knowing what you're looking for in a hurry is the best idea for an emergency. Oh, and don't forget to check and update your first aid kit regularly. You don't want to find yourself missing an item when you're in an emergency! It's important to keep the kit stocked up correctly.

Trivia #2

1. What is the purpose of first aid?

   A. To make people sick
   B. To help someone sick or injured until doctors or paramedics can take over
   C. To give someone a massage
   D. To teach people how to cook

2. What should you do if someone gets a scrape?

   A. Put ice on it
   B. Clean it with soap and water, then put a band-aid on it
   C. Ignore it and hope it goes away
   D. Give them a hug

3. What should you do if someone gets a bump on the head?

   A. Tell them to jump up and down
   B. Give them chocolate
   C. Tell them to sit or lie down, then put something cold on the bump

D. Ignore it and hope it goes away

4. What should you do if someone gets a nosebleed?

   A. Panic!
   B. Call their mum
   C. Pinch their nose hard
   D. Have them sit up straight and lean forward slightly

5. What should you do if someone gets burned?

   A. Cover it with a dirty cloth
   B. Leave the blisters alone
   C. Put ice on it
   D. Cover it with a clean, dry cloth or bandage after cooling it with cold water

6. What should you do if someone chokes?

   A. Encourage them to cough as hard as they can
   B. Tell them to take a nap
   C. Give them a piece of cake
   D. Ignore them

7. What should you do if someone gets lost in the wilderness?

   A. Panic and run around
   B. Make lots of noise to attract attention
   C. Sit down and cry
   D. Go to sleep

8. What is Morse code used for?

   A. Sending secret messages
   B. Ordering pizza

C. Playing games
D. Morse code is not used for anything

9. What should you do if you need clean water in the wild?

   A. Drink from any puddle you find
   B. Look for clear, flowing water
   C. Ask a wild animal for water
   D. Make your own water with magic

10. What is the purpose of a survival tin?

    A. To store cookies
    B. To build a spaceship
    C. To create a survival shelter
    D. To serve as a trusty, useful toolkit in the wilderness

First Aid & Emergency Care Crossword Puzzle

Embark on the First Aid & Emergency Care Crossword Puzzle! Can you fill in all the words related to first aid and emergency care? Put your knowledge to the test and see if you can solve the puzzle!

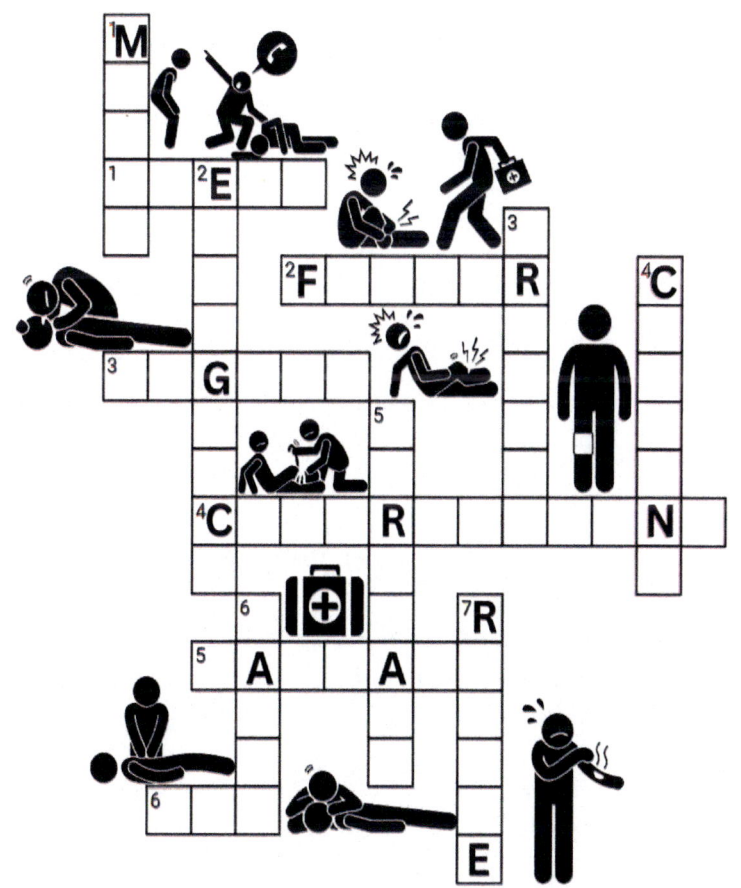

Across:

1. The area where an accident or emergency situation occurs
2. A device or method used to remove impurities from water
3. Actions or devices used to attract attention in an emergency
4. The action of pressing on a person's chest to help blood flow during CPR
5. A fabric strip used to cover and protect a wound
6. A life-saving procedure involving chest compressions and rescue breaths

Down:

1. A system of communication using dots and dashes
2. The process of providing assistance or relief to those in need during a crisis
3. The breaths given between chest compressions during CPR
4. A procedure to help a person who is choking
5. The immediate assistance given to an injured person
6. Essential for survival, it can be filtered from streams or collected from dew
7. A method of getting help by making noise or using visual signals

Section 3

STREET SMARTS

Fun Fact!

Did you know that carrying a whistle or safety alarm can help you stay safe in tricky situations? In this section, you'll learn how to use simple tools and smart strategies to navigate both busy city streets and remote villages, ensuring you're always prepared for any challenge!

How to Stay Safe in Tricky Situations!

Although we've been exploring the wilderness and surviving an outdoor adventure, there may be times when you need to be street savvy as you cross into cities, towns, or new neighborhoods.

When you enter more populated areas, you are more likely to meet more people, and while most people have good intentions, you can sometimes come across tricky behavior or people with unkind plans.

Here we'll deal with how to handle yourself, so that you can stay safe in tricky situations!

Humans have instincts for a reason, and if a situation feels threatening, then it perhaps is going to turn out that way. Do you ever feel like you have a little voice in your head saying: 'I don't feel okay here. I don't like this.' Then that little voice is perhaps a warning sign. It's your senses telling you that something is up, so listen to it.

Sticking with friends or family is the ideal solution to this. Whether you're on a remote island exploring, or playing in the street by your house, having family and friends watching over you makes all the difference.

When emerging into a busy, built-up area, such as city streets, populated areas, or roads, take extra care within your surroundings. Not only might the streets feel like a maze, but there might be moving vehicles, distractions, and more people to look out for. This is not the time to be looking down at a phone. Keep your eyes open!

As you walk around, take a 'mental note' of landmarks or places that will help you if you land up getting lost. It's likely you'll notice interesting things along the way, and this can be enjoyable! What tall buildings are around? What is the architecture like? Can you see anything you've never seen before?

Not only will this make your walk more intriguing, but it'll help you figure out your navigation safely.

You might meet some awesome people along the way, but you must always be aware of strangers. Not all strangers are bad, but it is smart to exercise caution with people that you don't know – even if they seem  super nice. When meeting new people, don't be afraid to say no, or to leave a situation if it feels tricky or is making you feel uncomfortable. A good person will understand that you are making a sensible decision to leave!

Don't forget to communicate, however. When you're out on the streets, or if you feel uncomfortable, then speak out! Keeping this sensation to yourself is no good. Find a trusted adult or find a place where reliable people are likely. Whether it be a nearby hospital, bus station, or police station, finding somewhere that 'feels' safe is vital.

Just to be on the safe side, you can be extra prepared for difficult situations by carrying a whistle or safety alarm. Then you can provide a 'BIG ALERT' noise should you find yourself in a bad spot!

And don't forget the things you already know, like wearing a helmet on a bike, wearing a seatbelt in a car, and not eating candy given by strangers.

Following this advice when venturing out on the streets means you'll be well equipped for almost anything. Trust your heart and head: they're often right about things.

Pro tip: Before heading into unfamiliar areas, agree with a friend or family member on regular check-in times. Send updates on your location and plans to ensure someone knows where you are and can act if you miss a check-in. 🌍📞

Stay Safe by City Streets

When traveling, if you go to a city, familiarize yourself with basic street signs and traffic signals. Know your road safety!

Depending on where you are in the world will depend on what sort of road-crossing advice you need to follow.

In the USA, find a designated crosswalk or intersection with pedestrian signals, then suss out the traffic! Have you heard the phrase 'stop, look, and listen?' This means that before stepping off the curb, look left, right, and then left again to check the coast is clear. Watch out for both vehicle traffic and cyclists.

Wait for the signal that shows 'walk'. Some signs say 'walk', while others might have a symbol of a person that turns green to signify that it is time for you to cross the road. Most intersections now have audible cues (like a beeping sound) to signal when you can cross.

If vehicles are approaching, make eye contact with the drivers if you can. This helps prevent accidents if you know that the driver has seen you. Remember: just because you can see them, doesn't always mean that they have seen you!

When you cross busy streets, always stay alert. While it might be tempting to listen to your favorite tune or check your phone, but use your senses effectively to remain safe. Listen to the traffic. Watch the road. Focus on your surroundings!

Pro tip:
Before heading into unfamiliar areas, agree with a friend or family member on regular check-in times. Send updates on your location and plans to ensure someone knows where you are and can act if you miss a check-in.

Stay Safe in a Remote Village

On the streets of a remote village, there might not be the hustle and bustle of busy traffic. So, what should you be looking out for instead? Well, different places around the world have different rules. There are customs and etiquettes, depending on different cultures and locations.

As you would anywhere else, stay aware of traffic and only cross a road when it is safe to do so. In far-flung parts of the planet, you might have to contend with wild animals, bikes, or other methods of transport crossing streets or pedestrian areas. Always keep your wits about you!

Depending on whether there are others around you, try to figure out what the local people are doing. How do they navigate life in their remote village? Learn about the culture before going to your destination, to truly master more rural and remote manners for staying safe on the street.

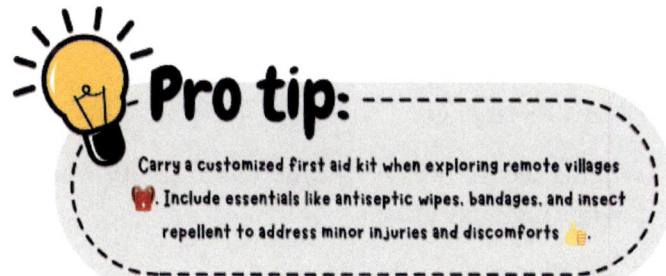

Pro tip: Carry a customized first aid kit when exploring remote villages 🎒. Include essentials like antiseptic wipes, bandages, and insect repellent to address minor injuries and discomforts 👍.

Trivia #3

1. When entering populated areas, what should you be mindful of?

    A. Empty roads
    B. Being helpful
    C. Ignoring your instincts
    D. Playing a card game

2. What does the little voice in your head serve as?

    A. An alarm clock
    B. A comforter
    C. A warning sign voice
    D. A GPS tracker

3. What is recommended for increased safety when navigating busy areas?

    A. Walking with eyes closed
    B. Wearing headphones
    C. Running across streets
    D. Keeping eyes open

4. What should you do to aid navigation in unfamiliar areas?

    A. Ignore landmarks
    B. Take a mental note of landmarks
    C. Keep eyes down
    D. Follow others blindly

5. When meeting new people, what should you be cautious of?

    A. Their fashion sense
    B. Their favorite color
    C. Their intentions
    D. Their age

6. What is suggested if you feel uncomfortable or unsafe?

    A. Communicate with a trusted adult
    B. Find a noisy place
    C. Keep sensations to yourself
    D. Laugh it off

7. How can you attract attention in a bad situation?

    A. Whispering
    B. Dancing
    C. Carrying a whistle or safety alarm
    D. Humming a tune

8. What are some general safety tips?

    A. Wear a helmet while sleeping
    B. Wear a seatbelt while walking
    C. Accept candy from strangers

D. Wear a helmet on a bike

9. What advice is given for crossing roads in a city?

   A. Look both ways
   B. Listen to music loudly
   C. Close your eyes
   D. Follow the crowd blindly

10. What is emphasized regarding trusting instincts?

    A. They are often wrong
    B. They are irrelevant
    C. They should be ignored
    D. They are often right

Street Smart Maze

Navigate through the Street Smarts Maze! Help the boy safely find his way through the city maze and back home. Can you guide him to the exit without getting lost?

Section 4

SURVIVING NATURAL DISASTERS

Fun Fact!

During a hurricane, if you find yourself outdoors and unable to find a building for shelter, seeking refuge in a ditch can actually be a safer option than being near trees or power lines. It might seem odd, but being in a lower, sturdy area can protect you from flying debris!

Surviving a Hurricane: A Kid's Guide

Hurricanes are mighty and strong winds.

If one heads your way, do you know how to handle it? Let's find out!

Before a storm hits, you'll usually have a warning: listen to the news or adults talking about bad weather on its way. An adult is likely to tell you that a hurricane is on its way!

If you're at home, gather supplies like water, food, and flashlights (don't forget replacement batteries) Have some of your favorite toys and games in the room with you, to keep you entertained. You'll need to stay indoors and check all windows and doors are tightly shut.

When the hurricane hits, stay calm and be with your family. Soothe and distract each other if family members are scared. You could use the opportunity to snuggle down together with blankets and a good book to take minds away from the sound outside. Listen to adults and follow instructions and local guidance.

After the storm passes, and you are told it is safe to do so, you might want to explore. You might see fallen power lines, large puddles, or fallen trees. Things might look different than they did before!

Check on your neighbors. See if anyone needs a helping hand.

If you happen to be outdoors on one of your big adventures when a hurricane hits, then you should seek shelter immediately. Look for somewhere sturdy as soon as you can. This could be a building, a designated storm shelter, or even a ditch if no other options are available. Avoid seeking shelter near trees, power lines, or other structures that could fall or be risky in high winds.

As the storm hits, you might find it beneficial to cover your head with your hands to protect yourself from flying debris. You could also use material or clothing to protect yourself from anything flying around in the hurricane! Aim to keep yourself as protected as possible!

Be mindful of rising water levels and potential flooding emerging nearby. Move to higher ground if you start to see water rising near you. Again, do your best to stay calm.

Hopefully, the storm will pass soon, young adventurer!

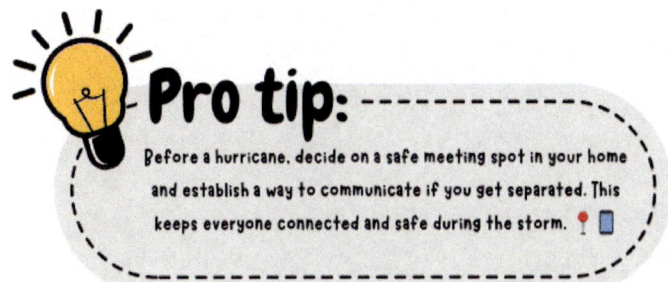

Pro tip: Before a hurricane, decide on a safe meeting spot in your home and establish a way to communicate if you get separated. This keeps everyone connected and safe during the storm. 🕯️📱

Surviving a Tornado: A Kid's Guide

The advice for surviving a tornado is similar to the hurricane, above. However, there are a few things to consider for a tornado specifically.

Think of a tornado as a huge spinning top that gathers speed in the sky. A tornado can form during stormy weather when warm air and cold air collide. When this happens, the wind begins to spin in a circle, hitting the ground and creating a tornado.

Some tornados are small – you might not even notice them. Some areas are prone to big tornados. For large tornados, aim for you and your family to head to an interior room or basement. If you're out and about, head towards the nearest sturdy building, and keep away from windows. Protect your head with your hands or a pillow. You could even wear your bike helmet for added protection!

Remain in your safe spot, staying calm, until the tornado passes. Once it has, then you can explore and check for any damage. Take care not to tread on any broken glass!

Check in on others, and make sure everyone is safe.

Pro tip:
🌪 Prepare a tornado emergency kit with bottled water, snacks, a flashlight with extra batteries, a first aid kit, and a whistle. This ensures you're ready if you need to shelter in place. 🔦🧰🛎

Surviving a Flood: What Kids Need to Know

When there is heavy rainfall, streets, and low-lying areas can quickly become flooded. Drainage systems may become overpowered, leading to water pooling on roads and sidewalks. Rivers and streams in the area can swell quite suddenly when there is lots of rain, and the water levels can burst their banks, affecting nearby homes, businesses, and farmland. This is how flooding starts.

Flooded roads are a problem for those on the road! Local authorities sometimes close roads during flooding seasons, or a road can quickly become impassable when drivers approach. Drivers must drop their speed before attempting to pass through any water level.

In severe flooding situations, residents might be told to evacuate their homes for safety. Sometimes, emergency shelters are opened to provide temporary housing for those relocated because of the floodwaters.

Flooding can be very upsetting when it causes extensive damage to homes, buildings, and belongings. Flooding can lead to expensive financial repairs!

When it comes to keeping yourself safe in a flood, listen to the adults and follow instructions. As a kid, you might find it fascinating to watch the water levels rising, but water is mighty! Water is more powerful than we often give it credit for.

If at risk of being caught by a flood, head to the highest point away from the area that might flood. You might need to leave your home or location, but don't panic - it doesn't always mean that your property will be affected! Sometimes, evacuation is a preventative measure (a 'just in case').

Wait in your safe place for the flood movement to settle, or the rainfall to fully pass, before heading back down to lower land or properties.

Be prepared for damage: when things get wet, they can break more easily – even if they are big objects like walls or structures! Always follow the instructions of trusted adults before heading back to an area that's been flooded.

Hopefully, you'll find all is safe and well when you return, young explorer!

Pro tip:
Before flood season, create a waterproof container for important documents like birth certificates, medical records, and emergency contact lists. Keeping these safe ensures you have essential information handy during and after a flood.

How to Survive a Tsunami

A tsunami is a gigantic wave: it's like something from a movie, yet it is a very serious and natural disaster. Perhaps you've seen the devastation of a tsunami on the news, or learned about one in a geography lesson?

A massive wave sounds cool, but tsunamis usually happen after something shifts or erupts under the water, like an earthquake or underwater volcano. When nature causes the ocean floor to shake or move, it can cause massive waves that travel swiftly across the ocean, sometimes even thousands of miles!

If you're ever near the ocean or at the beach when you see the water suddenly receding (going back) or you hear a roar like thunder, it could mean a tsunami is on the way.

Here's how to act:

1. Stay with your family or friends and aim to STAY CALM!
2. Head for high ground. If you're near the coast, get to higher ground and away from the water as soon as possible.
3. Follow the lead of the grown-ups.
4. Stay indoors away from windows until the tsunami warning is lifted.
5. Use radios, smartphones, or devices to stay informed with messages and updates via local

authorities or emergency services. (Where possible, use battery-powered devices because you might not have access to an electrical outlet. Plus, electrical outlets might be disrupted in poor conditions such as this).

6. Prepare that there may be other tsunami surges after the first one, so keep listening to the instructions from the authorities.
7. Once it is safe to leave, do so with caution and care, as there might be damage.

Tsunamis are powerful. They truly are a force of nature: we hope you stay safe!

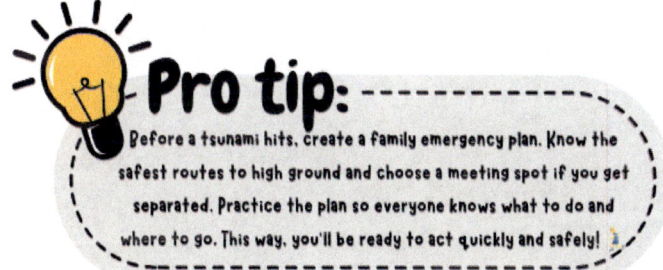

Pro tip: Before a tsunami hits, create a family emergency plan. Know the safest routes to high ground and choose a meeting spot if you get separated. Practice the plan so everyone knows what to do and where to go. This way, you'll be ready to act quickly and safely!

How to Survive an Earthquake

Do you understand what's happening in an earthquake?

Earthquakes happen when pieces of the Earth's crust, called tectonic plates, move and collide with each other.

The Earth's crust is made up of large pieces. You could look at it a bit like a giant jigsaw puzzle. Sometimes, the pieces naturally move around, and when they do, it can cause an earthquake. Sometimes, the movement will be triggered by things such as volcanic eruptions or disturbances.

When an earthquake hits, you might feel the ground shaking or rolling beneath your feet. The floor can feel like it's moving, and it can shake you around. It can shake objects and buildings around, too – if it's a bad one!

For earthquakes, the phrase to remember is: **'Drop, Cover, and Hold On'**.

If you're inside when the earthquake begins, drop to the ground, take cover under sturdy furniture or a door frame, and hold on tight (not too tight that you'll tire yourself out) until the shaking stops.

Stay away from items that might fall on you or break posing risk to you.

Wait for the earthquake to stop before leaving your safe spot!

If you're outside when an earthquake hits, and there's no time to reach indoors, still apply the 'Drop, Cover and Hold On' method.

But first, make sure you move to an open area. Head for somewhere like a field or a park, where there aren't structures nearby likely to squish you. It's also best to get out of panicked crowds or busy areas. Find space!

Drop to the ground and cover your head and neck with your arms to protect yourself from falling objects. Hold on to any nearby steady object, such as a bench or low wall. Stay put until the shaking stops. Assess if it is safe to move: stay alert to any further quakes or shakes. Listen to information or advice from local authorities or emergency services: they will tell you what to prepare for next!

Earthquakes can be tricky to predict! Scientists can forecast the likelihood of earthquakes occurring in certain places, but they cannot be definite on exact time and magnitude.

There are jobs specializing and developing our understanding of earthquakes. Is this something you would like to do? Researchers use data from seismographs, GPS measurements, and other monitoring tools to spot patterns and pinpoint areas at higher risk of earthquakes. This information helps everyone to prepare!

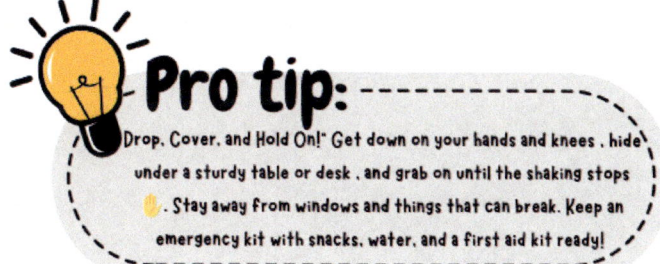

Pro tip: Drop, Cover, and Hold On!" Get down on your hands and knees, hide under a sturdy table or desk, and grab on until the shaking stops 🖐. Stay away from windows and things that can break. Keep an emergency kit with snacks, water, and a first aid kit ready!

How to Avoid Being Struck by Lightning

We know you're a brave explorer who perhaps enjoys watching a crazy storm! Have you ever seen hair-raising fork lightning slash towards the ground? Would you get a thrill out of super loud claps of thunder nearby?

If you're outdoors and hear thunder or see lightning, head for shelter – even if you think the storm looks rather awesome! Avoid seeking shelter under trees or in exposed areas.

To lower your risk of being struck by lightning indoors, avoid touching windows, and anything that conducts electricity (electrical appliances conduct electricity).

Wait! The storm will pass. It's best to wait around half an hour after the last thunderclap before heading back outdoors or moving forward on your adventure.

When lightning occurs, certainly don't go swimming! And it's definitely not time to take a bath! Water conducts electricity well (which means it attracts the electric current and can pose a significant risk – yikes!)

Should you have nowhere indoors to hide out in a lightning storm, then crouch down on the balls of your feet, with your feet close together. You can put your hands over your ears, too. Don't lay flat on the ground, as this increases the risk of a current from the lightning passing through your body.

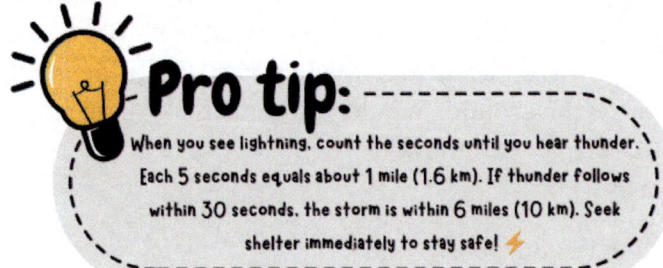

Pro tip: When you see lightning, count the seconds until you hear thunder. Each 5 seconds equals about 1 mile (1.6 km). If thunder follows within 30 seconds, the storm is within 6 miles (10 km). Seek shelter immediately to stay safe! ⚡

Cool Craft: Make a Tornado in a Bottle!

A real-life tornado sounded pretty scary, didn't it? In fact, all of these natural elements pose risks and danger to human life, but that doesn't stop us from being intrigued and in awe of them. To safely enjoy these wild weather types, you can do experiments at home to understand them better (on a small, much less dangerous scale!)

Let's look at how you can do a cool craft and make a tornado in a bottle.

Here's what you'll need:

- Two clear plastic bottles with caps
- Water
- Dish/washing up soap/liquid
- Optional: Glitter or food coloring (if you want a visual effect)

What to do:

1. Using water, fill one of the plastic bottles about three-quarters full.
2. Add a few drops of dish/washing up soap to the water. The soapiness will help make bubbles, so the tornado is easier to see.

3. If desired, add a touch of glitter or a few drops of food coloring to the water. This will also help to make your tornado more visible.
4. Tightly screw the cap onto the bottle filled with water and soap.
5. Next, take the second empty plastic bottle and turn it upside down. Put it on top of the first bottle: you want it so that the 'mouths' of the two bottles are touching.
6. Hold the two bottles together firmly (perhaps get an adult to do this bit), then quickly flip them over.
7. Now, the empty bottle should be on the bottom, while the bottle with water and soap is on the top.
8. Swirl both bottles in a circular motion for a few seconds, then stop and watch. You should catch sight of a mini tornado forming inside the bottle filled with water and soap! Enjoy!

How does *that* work?

When swirling the bottles, you are creating a vortex in the same way that a swirling tornado is a vortex (a twister or whirlpool motion).

Trivia #4

1. What natural disaster is the focus of the passage "Surviving a Hurricane: A Kid's Guide"?

    A. Earthquake
    B. Hurricane
    C. Tornado
    D. Tsunami

2. What should you gather at home before a hurricane hits?

    A. Water, food, and flashlights
    B. Sports equipment
    C. Your favorite toy
    D. Electronics and gadgets

3. What is the recommended action if you're outdoors during a hurricane?

    A. Climb a tree for safety
    B. Seek shelter under a big tree
    C. Stay in an open field
    D. Seek shelter in a sturdy building or ditch

4. How should you protect yourself from flying debris during a hurricane?

   A. Use an umbrella
   B. Cover your head with your hands or material
   C. Wear cool sunglasses
   D. Stand close to windows

5. What is the primary advice for surviving a tornado mentioned in the guide?

   A. Stay near windows
   B. Head to the basement or interior room
   C. Move into the tornado's path
   D. Climb to the rooftop

6. In the event of a flood, what should you do to keep yourself safe?

   A. Dip your hand in the water
   B. Head to lower ground
   C. Stay indoors and wait for the water to come in
   D. Head to the highest point away from the flood area

7. If by the ocean, how might you identify a potential tsunami on its way?

   A. Sudden heavy rainfall
   B. Roaring sound like thunder
   C. Bright sunshine
   D. Gentle ocean waves

8. What should you do if you hear thunder or see lightning while outdoors?

    A. Seek shelter under trees
    B. Stay near water
    C. Head indoors to a safe location
    D. Climb to the top of a hill

9. What is the recommended safety measure during a lightning storm if you have nowhere indoors to hide?

    A. Lay flat on the ground
    B. Stand tall and wave your arms
    C. Crouch down on the balls of your feet with hands over your ears
    D. Walk around singing a song

10. What is the suggested material to use to protect your head and neck during an earthquake?

    A. A bicycle helmet
    B. A paper bag
    C. A plastic bottle
    D. A wooden plank

Surviving Natural Disasters Word Search Puzzle

Prepare for the Surviving Natural Disasters Word Search Puzzle! Can you locate all the hidden words related to surviving natural disasters? Put your knowledge to the test and uncover them all!

```
T Q H T N J J E G E I L T R R F Q Q F R
S G I Y O C V M G R E S C U E X K P U F
N T G G A F L A C I O B S Q S B C U L L
O E H F H A M B S E O K F W O Z G A Z O
I E G R C A O A T U W H I U G R H E X O
T B R Y D W I A Z E R G U S T D N U S D
C F O P Z S U T W N R V W U Q T X S I I
U R U K T C H Y Y F A Z I Y L R N C F E
R J N N A S T E C R D L B V E E E A N K
T I D V J E U G R H Z C L T E D M W G W
S P E T F X I N G L O V F F I S L A Y
N F J A J B M I A Q D E G U L E O T N C
I C S D U N R N M M H E R Y Z D E I E N
S B C X F K O R Q S I X Q Q A R E J K E
F T Y F F A T A D E L X D N R B P V G G
E J J N B I S W I U K E R M J Z Y Y Z R
L A V I V R U S O A O O R T Z D O U M E
Y Z T U E K A U Q H T R A E W G I Q H M
N B D U X J E L I G H T N I N G I J V E
Z S E D U H U R R I C A N E T D O V M S
```

CALM
DAMAGE
EARTHQUAKE
EMERGENCY
EVACUATE
FAMILY

FLOOD
HIGHGROUND
HURRICANE
INSTRUCTIONS
LIGHTNING
RESCUE

SAFETY
SHELTER
STORM
SURVIVAL
SURVIVE
TORNADO

TSUNAMI
WARNING
WATER

Section 5

HUMAN HAZARDS

Fun Fact!

Did you know that some electric cars have windows that automatically roll down when they detect they're underwater? This cool feature helps passengers escape quickly in case the car goes for an unexpected swim!

How to Escape from a Burning Building

FIRE! GET OUT!

Fire drills start when you're young; you may have experienced a fire drill at school. That's because knowing how to escape from a burning building is a critical skill. Everyone should learn how to do it.

If you see, smell or suspect fire, raise the alarm as soon as you can. Alert others. Smoke should also raise the alarm for everybody to hear. If you see fire and the alarm isn't going off (or if you're outside with no fire alarm!) start shouting loudly to ensure people can hear; encourage others to do the same. Shout: "Fire!" at the top of your voice.

"FIRE!" Why not have a quick practice shout now?

If indoors, find the nearest exit. Evacuate the building via the quickest exit route and use stairs instead of elevators. There's a chance that an elevator may stop working if fire hits it before you get out.

If you are near the fire, or you can smell fire in the air, stay close to the ground. By doing this, you are where the air is clearer, which will help you breathe more easily.

It's also a great idea to cover your mouth to reduce smoke inhalation and toxic fumes. Use a piece of clothing to cover your nose and mouth until you're safely away from the fire.

If everything goes dark before you've left the building (which can sometimes happen if a fire makes the lighting system malfunction) then carefully feel your way along the floor or the wall. Close doors behind you as you go because this will prolong the spread of fire for a little longer.

Once outside and at a safe distance away from the burning building, await the emergency services, and quietly wait for instructions from adults or those in charge.

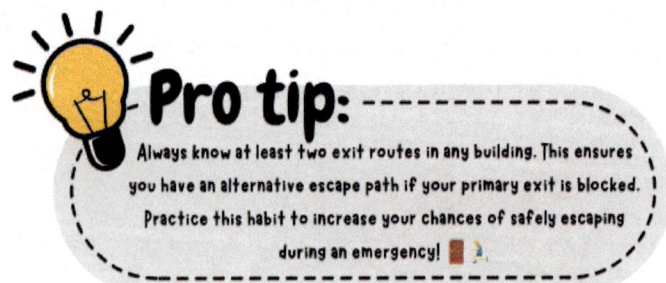

Pro tip: Always know at least two exit routes in any building. This ensures you have an alternative escape path if your primary exit is blocked. Practice this habit to increase your chances of safely escaping during an emergency!

How to Survive Being Trapped in a Car Going Underwater

Have you ever fancied the idea of going in a submarine? What about a submerged, sinking car? Probably not the latter option! It's an unlikely scenario for most people, but let's explore what to do should you find that you're the unlucky one in a car taking an unexpected dunking trip.

As usual, try to stay calm, as this will better help you to think properly and act! You've got to respond quickly: think of yourself as a speedy superhero, quick as a flash. Once a car hits the water, you've only got a couple of minutes before the water will have filled up the inside, so don't hang about.

Break out of your seatbelt. If you've got time to do so, unwind the windows promptly – this is your escape route. Get out of the car as fast as a bullet, and swim out of the water.

You might be thinking... what about the doors? Of course, try the door first, but many cars have locking features, and you'll find that once the car is in the water, the doors won't open (the force of the water will be nearly impossible to push). Plus, if you think about it, the doors will let in a HUGE amount of water. You might sink even faster if you open the doors, so windows are your best option.

If you find that a window is not opening for you, you're going to need to do something really risky... you're going to need to smash through the window to get out. Some cars come with an object or hammer specifically for this safety feature, but lots of cars won't have this to hand; you might need to use your imagination and find the heaviest thing you can inside the car to smash the window.

Once you're out, and you've reached the surface of the water, send your stress signals! Let people know you're in deep water (excuse the pun). People around need to know that you're in trouble and raise the alarm with the emergency services!

Head to a safe spot and await help. Take deep breaths, especially if you've been in the water. If you're very cold from the water, move around to keep warm or someone may provide you with dry clothing or a blanket.

Stay warm and wait for help. Don't make any attempt to rescue the sinking car. If the people are safe on land, then that's what matters.

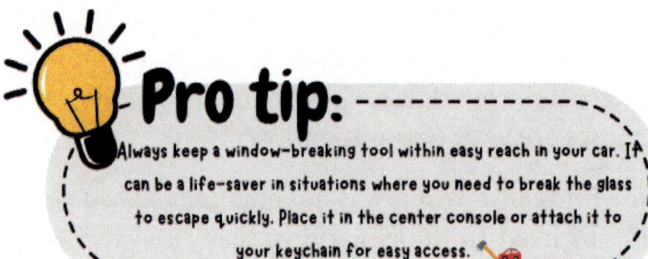

Pro tip: Always keep a window-breaking tool within easy reach in your car. It can be a life-saver in situations where you need to break the glass to escape quickly. Place it in the center console or attach it to your keychain for easy access.

Escaping the Elevator: What to Do When You're Stuck

For your next set of superhero tricks, how about escaping an elevator?

For many people, getting stuck in an elevator is their worst nightmare, but with our handy guide, you'll know exactly what to do should this happen to you.

Let's pretend you're traveling from Floor 100 down to Floor 1, when suddenly the elevator stops. It's not moving. You wait, and it's still not moving. You feel worried. Your palms start to sweat, and your heart is beating fast.

Take a deep breath. First things first, press every single button in the elevator. See if can get anything moving. Still not working? Look for the 'alarm' button. Elevators are fitted with alarm systems, so press this to raise the signal that you are stuck inside. In addition, some elevators also have phone numbers or 'emergency lines' visible for you to make a phone call. Some elevators have a phone inside them for this very reason. If you have a phone and you have a signal, then you can also call the emergency services who can send someone on their way.

Whilst you wait to be set free, distract yourself so that panic doesn't set in. Are there other people in the elevator with you? If so, now is the time to make new friends!

Together, you could also try shouting out to see if someone can hear you.

If you are alone, try some mediation-style techniques to remain calm. Count different items – buttons, ceiling tiles, spots on the floor – to take your mind off the situation until someone can swoop in and save you.

Someone will show up if you've raised the alarm and made plenty of noise. Stick it out and wait for your elevator rescue!

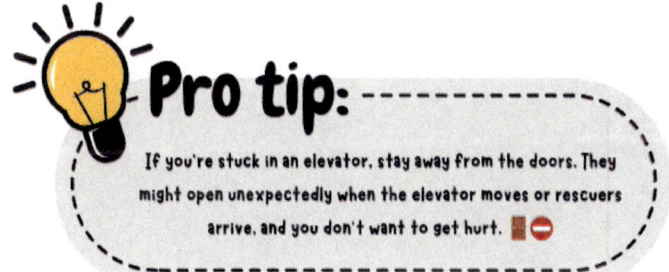

Pro tip:
If you're stuck in an elevator, stay away from the doors. They might open unexpectedly when the elevator moves or rescuers arrive, and you don't want to get hurt.

Caught in a Rip Tide: How to Stay Safe in Strong Currents

The beach is a fantastic place to spend time, especially on a sunny day when you catch a chance to splash about in the waves. Lots of people love a sea swim, too. Perhaps you're out floating on your back in the glorious water when... uh-oh! Suddenly, you find yourself caught in a rip tide – it's like being caught in a speeding river that is set to take you where it wants.

A rip tide happens from a strong, narrow current of water forming. Rip tides typically form at breaks near piers, or around jetties, where there's a lot of water movement.

Wind can also influence the way that the waves move, and wind can change suddenly. Conditions can quickly become open to rip currents.

If you feel that you're being pulled away from the shore in a rip tide, float on your back like a starfish. Spread your arms and legs like you're doing a snow angel and remain as calm as possible. The water will move you, but the chances are that it will carry you beyond the breaking waters.

Fighting the water will only land you in exhaustion, and you aren't likely to win against a rip tide (however strong you think you are). Water is so powerful that you must work with it. You quite literally need to 'go with the flow' on this one.

Make sure you signal for help by raising your arms and shouting 'Help!' Rip tides aren't always visible, especially from the shore, so you must call for help to avoid anyone thinking you're just choosing to float along in the water.

When you feel the rip tide losing its grip on you, swim parallel to the shore to get free of the most powerful part of the water. Once you feel you can control your swimming in calm water, then swim back to land, and seek assistance.

Beaches and waters likely to have riptides tend to have flags or warning signs, so always look out for these before entering water. Some places will also have lifeguards on the lookout. However, it is your responsibility to take care, so aim to swim only if you know the water is safe, open, and in sight of others watching out for you.

Now go ahead and enjoy your beach day, water warrior!

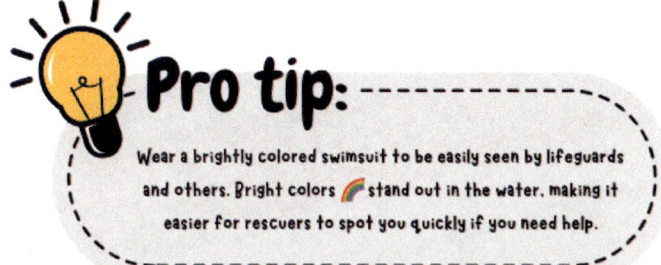

Pro tip:
Wear a brightly colored swimsuit to be easily seen by lifeguards and others. Bright colors stand out in the water, making it easier for rescuers to spot you quickly if you need help.

Cool Craft:
Create an Emergency Escape Plan

Why not use your newfound knowledge to put together a leaflet or brochure to 'map out' an emergency escape plan for you and your family and friends? This is a straightforward and fun crafting activity to put your knowledge to the test!

Start by conjuring the different types of emergencies that could happen in your area. Perhaps include fires, earthquakes, severe storms, or any other natural disasters. In your escape plan, explain what each emergency entails and how people should respond.

Draw a floor plan of your home, including rooms, doors, windows, and possible exits. Add an arrow if you want to show the easiest ways to exit! Make sure you mark out a few exit routes in case you need to use 'Plan B' in an emergency.

Mark a meeting point. Write down or draw a big X at the point in which you and your family could meet and agree upon a point of safety. It might be the top of a driveway, by the neighbor's house, or at the mailbox. Make sure everybody in the house will be able to identify your safety checkpoint.

In your guide, label and explain different methods of escape. Remember how escaping a burning building might be different from staying safe in a hurricane. Include clear instructions in your handy escape plan.

If you've already prepared an emergency or first-aid kit somewhere in your house, include how to find it. Anyone who picks up your emergency escape plan can then read how to find these survival essentials!

And don't forget something very important to add to your escape plan: emergency phone numbers! Perhaps use bright, bold colors to write the emergency numbers on your plan, leaflet, or guide.

Home layouts can change, and new hazards may emerge, so keep your plan up-to-date.

Review and edit it every so often.

Once you're done, share your emergency plan with your family and friends! Well done for crafting such an important document!

Trivia #5

1. What should you do if you encounter a fire indoors?

    A. Run around in panic
    B. Stay close to the fire to keep warm
    C. Find the nearest exit and evacuate the building
    D. Ignite more objects in the building

2. What action should you take if you're trapped in a car sinking underwater?

    A. Stay calm and wait for help
    B. Open the doors immediately
    C. Break the windows to escape
    D. Secure yourself with the seatbelt

3. What's the first thing to do if you're stuck in an elevator?

    A. Panic and scream for help
    B. Try to open the doors forcefully
    C. Cry
    D. Remain calm and press the alarm button

4. How should you signal for help if caught in a rip tide?

    A. Wave and shout "Yay, I'm swimming!"
    B. Raise your arms and shout "Help!"
    C. Be silent and float around
    D. Splash water around to get attention

5. What's the recommended way to escape a burning building?

    A. Use the elevator
    B. Stay close to the ceiling
    C. Evacuate via the nearest exit
    D. Remain where you are and wait for firefighters

6. What should you do to stay calm while stuck in an elevator?

    A. Start jumping to get attention
    B. Smash things
    C. Use your best singing voice
    D. Use meditation techniques

7. What should you do if you smell smoke in a building?

    A. Keep quiet and ignore it
    B. Quickly exit the building through any door
    C. Search for the source of the smell
    D. Inform others and evacuate following the nearest exit

8. How can you increase your chances of being rescued if trapped in a car underwater?

    A. Roll down the windows and stay in the car
    B. Remain still and wait for help
    C. Break the windows and swim to the surface
    D. Turn on the radio

9. What's the recommended position to adopt if caught in a rip tide?

    A. Float on your back and remain calm
    B. Face down and front crawl
    C. Dive deep underwater to escape the current
    D. Eat seaweed

10. What's the primary purpose of an emergency escape plan?

    A. To increase the chance of encountering emergencies
    B. To create confusion among family members
    C. To provide clear instructions for safe evacuation
    D. To demonstrate firefighting techniques

Human Hazards Crossword Puzzle

Challenge yourself with the Human Hazards Crossword Puzzle! Can you fill in all the words related to potential dangers posed by humans? Test your knowledge and see if you can solve the puzzle!

Across

1. What should you try to open to escape from a sinking car?
2. What might you be stuck in if it stops moving between floors
3. What emergency situation requires immediate evacuation?
4. What action should you take if you're in a dangerous situation?
5. What should you do to attract attention if you're in distress?
6. What situation are you in if your car is submerged in water?
7. What vehicle might you be trapped in if it goes underwater?
8. What safer alternative should you use instead of elevators during an evacuation
9. What indicates the presence of fire in a building?

Down

1. What should you use to protect your nose and mouth from smoke?
2. What word means to leave a building quickly and safely during an emergency?
3. What do you look for to leave a building during a fire?
4. What should you do loudly to alert others in an emergency?
5. What type of situation requires quick action and assistance?
6. What can happen if the lighting system malfunctions during a fire?

7. Where should you stay close to if you're near a fire to breathe more easily?
8. What device alerts people about a fire or emergency?

Section 6

ANIMAL DANGERS

Fun Fact!

Did you know that snakes can "hear" through their jaws? Unlike humans, snakes don't have external ears. Instead, they sense vibrations through the ground with their jawbones, helping them detect potential prey or threats nearby! So, if you're walking in a snake-prone area, those slithering creatures might actually "hear" you coming long before you see them!

SSSSSnake Encounters

How do you feel about snakes? These slithering creatures can be a bit of a conversation divider: people either like them or loathe them. Some people are afraid of snakes having never even encountered one before.

Snakes are often more scared of humans than we are of them, so if you're out exploring and you see a snake, it's best to leave them be. The snake is likely just doing its own thing, enjoying itself. It probably doesn't want a human approaching it!

Snakes will likely slither away if given the chance. Backing away slowly can help create space without startling or bothering the snake.

You should never try to touch or handle a snake, even if it looks harmless and lovely. Some types of snakes can be venomous, which means that their bite or venom can make humans very sick. Rarely, some snake venoms can be fatal (causing death). A few snake breeds can become aggressive when provoked, so it's best to just admire them from a safe distance.

To be more mindful of snakes, watch your step! In areas where snakes might be hiding, such as tall grass, bushes, or under rocks, stick to clear pathways to avoid stepping on an unsuspecting snake.

If you do find yourself close to a snake, then avoid being near its head. If a snake feels threatened, it may defensively strike out to bite. Treat the snake's space with respect!

When it comes to snakes, every great explorer knows their creatures. Scrub up and research what types of snakes you might find in the area where you are going. Learn about snakes: take time to find out about the different types of snakes that you might encounter. By doing this, you'll be well-educated on how to behave around these slithering friends.

From afar, snakes are beautiful creatures to watch in their natural habitats. They're quick, too – so watch out!

Pro tip:

When exploring snake habitats, wear boots and long pants. This protects you from accidental snake bites if you get too close. Stay safe on your adventure!

Bear Encounter Escape Guide: Be Bear Aware!

North America, western regions of Canada, and the United States are typically home to grizzly bears. Grizzly bears inhabit various habitats, including forests, mountains, and meadows.

Grizzly bears prefer hanging out in areas with good food sources (who doesn't!), where they have lots of access to berries, nuts, roots, insects, and occasionally larger prey like fish and mammals. Have you ever felt as 'hungry as a bear?'

These bears are known for their distinctive hump on their shoulders and their silver-tipped fur. While their appearance seems soft, cuddly, and beautiful, these creatures are not teddy bears!

If you find a grizzly bear, remain calm and avoid panicking. Bears can sense fear and may become more aggressive if they perceive you as a threat.

Don't run! Running can trigger a bear's instinct to chase, which is their natural predatory behavior. Instead, stand your ground and avoid making sudden movements. Running away can make the situation worse, so if anything, back away very slowly.

Look around and consider the situation and your surroundings. If the bear is unaware of your presence or seems indifferent, you could back away slowly without disturbing it.

If the bear has locked eyes on you, speak calmly and firmly to let it know you are human.

Avoid making direct eye contact, as this can be perceived as a threat: perhaps look slightly to the left or right of the bear, or focus on an object while keeping the bear in your peripheral (outer) vision. Slowly wave your arms to make yourself appear larger. If you appear larger than the bear, it is less likely to approach you.

Do not turn your back on the bear until you are a safe distance away.

In areas where you are expecting there to be bears, it's a wise move to carry 'bear spray' in your backpack. If the bear charges or shows signs of aggression, use bear spray if you have it. Bear spray can discourage a charging bear and give you time to slowly back away to safety. Follow the instructions on the canister for use (ideally read the instructions before going out into the area with bears! You don't want to be reading a full set of instructions when facing up to a bear!)

If a grizzly bear attacks you, your best option may be to play dead. Yes, this sounds scary, and you'll need to keep your cool and hold your nerve! Lie flat on your stomach with your hands clasped behind your neck to protect yourself. Keep your legs spread apart to make it more difficult for the bear to flip you over. Stay still. Avoid screaming or moving until the bear leaves the area.

After an encounter with a grizzly bear, report it to the local wildlife authorities or park rangers. They can assess the situation and take appropriate measures for the future and safety of others.

If you understand bears and their behavior, you have a far better chance of staying safe around them. Read up on these awesome animals before you enter any potential bear habitat.

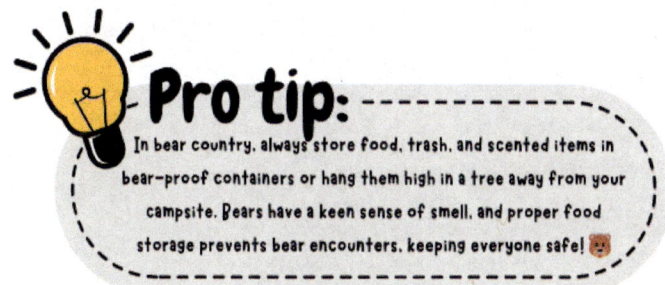

Pro tip: In bear country, always store food, trash, and scented items in bear-proof containers or hang them high in a tree away from your campsite. Bears have a keen sense of smell, and proper food storage prevents bear encounters, keeping everyone safe! 🐻

Bee Encounter Escape Guide: Buzzing Away Safely!

In nature, you might stumble across a bee's nest in a tree or a nook – bees like secret hideouts and places with luscious greenery. Should you accidentally approach a bee's nest, stay cool. Bees sense when humans are feeling nervous.

Instead of making a mad dash screaming: "BEEEEEEEE!", take it slow and steady. Gently move away from the bee nest; you could even tiptoe away quietly. If you're anxious about getting stung, use your hands or clothes to cover your face and head. These body parts are the bits that hurt most following a bee sting: it's not pleasant to be stung.

Very rarely, if bees feel threatened, they may create a swarm. It can be tempting to start swatting your hands to get a group of bees away, but doing so might land you with even more stings than you bargained for. Leave them bee (geddit?), if possible.

If you do get stung, gently scrape out the stinger with your fingernail or a card. Avoid squeezing, as this might make the venom feel a little worse!

Some people are allergic to bee stings, so keep an eye out for any signs of allergic reactions, like swelling or trouble breathing. If you or a friend starts showing signs of a reaction, find an adult! Beeee quick!

After buzzing away to safety, tell grown-ups about the bee nest. They can then report it and sort out the situation.

Bees are awesome. Bees are also vital to nature.

Bees are master pollinators, as they transfer pollen from one flower to another, fertilizing plants and enabling them to produce fruits, vegetables, nuts, and seeds.

Did you know: bees are responsible for pollinating over 75% of the world's leading food crops? How hungry we might be without bees!

Bees also support a variety of ecosystems and sustain plants and wildlife. Bees are crucial to many crops, which leads to boosting economics (money). And, of course, we can't mention bees without talking about honey! Bees produce delicious honey, so let's aim to leave them BEE (we just can't help ourselves, can we?) They are busy. Don't disturb any nest full of busy, buzzy beeeeees…

Pro tip: Avoid using strong perfumes, lotions, or wearing brightly colored clothing outdoors. 🐝🌺 Bees are attracted to floral scents and vibrant colors, so staying low-key can help you avoid unexpected bee encounters! 🚶🛡️

Spider Encounter Survival Guide: Greeting Venomous Spiders!

Whether you're an arachnid enthusiast or a fearful friend of the spider, encountering venomous spiders requires knowledge and know-how. You might not mean to stumble across a spider, or should that be… a spider might not mean to stumble across YOU?

Did you know that there are over 45,000 species of spiders globally? From colorful jumping spiders to the mysterious black widows, spiders are different and varied. Some are harmless. Some are venomous.

Know this: most spiders pose no threat to humans whatsoever. Only a small percentage of spider species are venomous, and even fewer have venom powerful enough to cause harm to humans. So, before you start screaming at the sight of a spider, take a moment to consider these creatures as part of nature. Spiders are part of the ecosystem, and they want you to leave them alone. They're not here to frighten you!

If you come across a spider and want to know whether it is venomous or not, there are some telltale signs to look out for. Venomous spiders often have distinct patterns or colors. If you're not sure, continue to admire from a safe distance. The spider doesn't really want you to disturb it, after all!

Did you know that black widow spiders are relatively small? The males and females usually look a bit different, with the female usually jet black and shiny, while the male might have lighter or browner colorings. One of the most  recognizable features of the female black widow spider is the red hourglass marking on the underside of the abdomen (although we don't recommend touching a spider to turn it upside down to look!). The hourglass marking is typically bright red – red being the warning color. That's your big hint to stay away.

Let's say you've spotted a venomous spider—now what? Avoid making sudden movements or loud noises that could startle or provoke the spider. Back away from the 8-legged territory.

In the unlikely event that you need to handle a venomous spider, exercise caution and follow these expert-only spider-handling tips:

- Wear thick gloves or use a container with card to avoid touching the spider. You can scoop it up and take it outdoors – only if you need to and you're careful. (Get an adult to do this).
- Keep a safe distance from the spider's fangs to avoid getting bitten.

- Transport the spider to a suitable habitat away – somewhere it can be left alone to weave its web and make a new, comfy home.
- Get help if you or someone else is bitten by a venomous spider. Don't delay. It's better to be safe than sorry! While most spider bites are harmless and cause only mild irritation, some venomous species can cause more serious symptoms, such as pain, swelling, nausea, or difficulty breathing. Your local emergency service will tell you what to do, and what symptoms to look out for next.

Spiders often have a bad reputation (so many people hate spiders, huh!?) But spiders play an important role in maintaining the balance of ecosystems around the world. Next time you see a spider, think about how it's just doing its job.

It's not out to get you!

Pro tip: Keep your living spaces clutter-free and seal cracks or gaps where spiders might enter. 🕷️✨ Regularly dust and vacuum to remove webs and egg sacs. By maintaining a tidy environment, you reduce the likelihood of unexpected spider encounters indoors! 🏠

Sting and Bite Guide: Heal the Hurt!

Ouch! Getting stung or bitten can hurt. Not only that, but it can temporarily damage the skin or inflict a reaction so let's learn how to heal the hurt and handle the situation.

Depending on what you've been stung or bitten by will depend on how to treat the minor ailment. Our handy guide will deal with different types of stings and bites:

Bee Stings

If you've been stung by a bee, the first step is to remove the stinger. Use tweezers or your fingernail to carefully scrape the stinger out of your skin. Scraping is better than squeezing, as squeezing stands the chance of putting more venom into your skin, making it sting even more!

After removing the stinger, wash the area with soap and water to prevent infection of the skin. If available, apply a cold compress or ice pack to reduce swelling and ease pain. With an adult's advice, you might also take pain relief to help reduce the swelling and handle the discomfort.

If you experience signs of an allergic reaction, seek medical attention immediately. Allergic reaction signs include sudden swelling, breathlessness, significant rashes, or anything else you think might suggest a person's body is reacting badly or struggling.

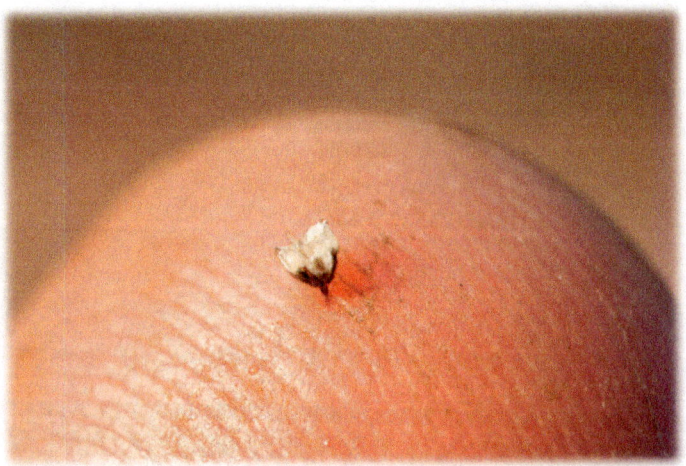

Spider Bites

Spider bites depend on how severe the bite is, and the individual who has been bitten. Some people's bodies react differently to others. What might cause a reaction in one person, might not affect the next person.

If you are bitten by a spider, wash the bite area with soap and water to clean the wound. This will also alleviate the risk of getting infected. You can also apply a cold compress or ice pack to help the swelling go down and to take some pain away.

Try to keep the affected body part elevated to help reduce swelling and promote good blood circulation.

If you are concerned that the spider may be venomous or if you experience symptoms such as severe pain, swelling, redness, or feeling/being sick, seek medical attention straight away.

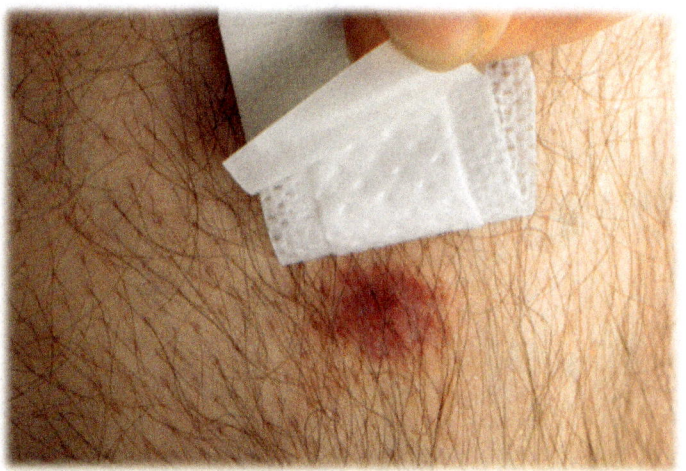

Mosquito Bites

Annoying mosquitoes can leave behind itchy, red bites. It's hard not to scratch them, huh? However, it is best not to. Scratching tends to make the bites worse, and extreme scratching can cause the skin to bleed.

Wash the bite area with soap and water to reduce the risk of infection.

With an adult's support, you can apply an antihistamine cream or calamine lotion to help reduce itching and inflammation.

Also under adult direction, you might take an oral antihistamine to help reduce the irritation of mosquito bites. Mosquito bites tend to occur in warmer climates, and sometimes people are more prone to them at night. In places where mosquito bites are very likely, you can buy mosquito nets to protect you while you sleep. These nets go around your bed.

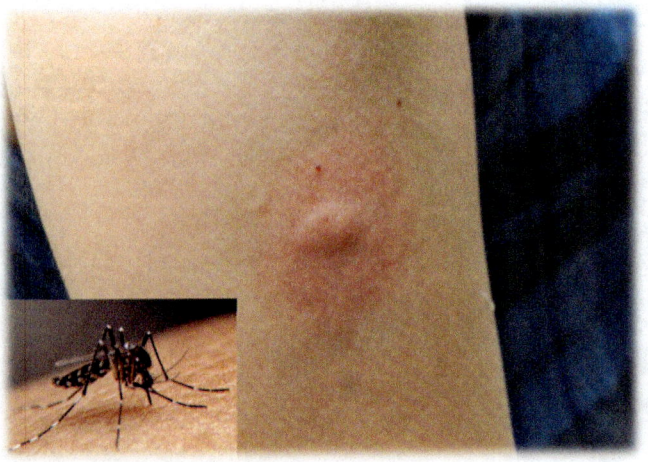

Tick Bites

Tick bites have the potential to transmit diseases like Lyme disease, so it's essential to remove ticks promptly, and then monitor for any signs of infection.

If you've been bitten by a tick, use tweezers to grasp the tick as close to the skin's surface as possible.

Taking care, gently pull upward with steady, even pressure to remove the tick from the skin. Don't twist or jerk suddenly, as this can cause the tick's mouthparts to break off and remain embedded in the skin. Yuck!

When you've got the tick out, wash and clean the area. Use an antiseptic wipe to cleanse, too.

Keep an eye on yourself or the person bitten for a couple of days. Should there be any cold of flu-like symptoms, you'll need to check in with a medical professional.

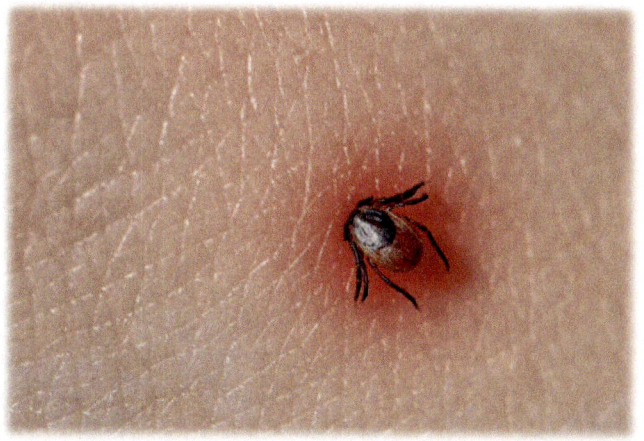

With all of the above in mind, there's lots you can do to prevent insect stings and bites. Wear insect repellent and wear long sleeves if you can. Carry insect repellent and creams just in case. Always be prepared, great adventurer!

Despite there being bugs and beasties outdoors, don't let it stop you. Enjoy the outdoors, enjoy your adventures, and enjoy the wonders of nature – big and small.

Pro tip: After a sting or bite, apply a cool, damp cloth directly to the affected area. This reduces swelling and provides immediate relief. Keep a small, damp cloth or cold pack handy in your outdoor kit for quick soothing!

Cool Craft: Build a Bug House or Hotel

Have you ever thought of decorating your own house? What about an awesome hotel with lots of rooms where you can truly put your hosting skills to the test?

Well, now you can… on a small scale. For this cool craft, you can make a bug house or hotel for the insects and beasties out there! Follow our tips, and you might well be lucky enough to experience some visiting bugs!

What you'll need for this project:

- A sturdy wooden or plastic box with a lid (cardboard will break if it gets wet)
- Some soil
- Rocks or pebbles
- Some small twigs, branches, and leaves
- Optional decorations like stickers, fake plants, miniature furniture, or toy insects – for fun!

What to do:

Select a suitable container for your Bug House or Bug Hotel. Choose something that won't fall apart when exposed to the outdoor elements! And remember, bugs might visit the house to stay out of the weather…

Line the bottom of the box with a layer soil to create a comfortable flooring for the bugs. You can then add rocks or pebbles for drainage and texture.

Arrange twigs, branches, and leaves so that bugs have somewhere to hide. Think of these items like furniture for bugs… or a bed! Everyone likes a bed – even a tiny bug.

You could further decorate and personalize with finishing touches to your Bug Box House. You could add stickers, fake plants, miniature furniture, or toy insects. Get creative and make it look appealing and fun.

You might need to wait a few hours, or days, to see if any bugs decide to come to your 'Bug House' for a rest. Keep your eye on what you've made.

Pull up your front-row seat to nature's friends!

Trivia #6

1. What should you do if you encounter a snake while exploring in nature?

    A. Approach it slowly because it wants to be your friend
    B. Try to touch or handle it
    C. Back away slowly
    D. Run away as fast as you can

2. Which North American region is typically home to grizzly bears?

    A. Western Canada and the United States
    B. Southern United States
    C. Eastern Canada
    D. Midwest United States

3. What food sources do grizzly bears prefer?

    A. Berries, nuts, roots, and insects
    B. Meat only
    C. Leaves and grass
    D. Fish and aquatic plants

4. How should you behave if you encounter a grizzly bear?

   A. Run away as fast as you can
   B. Speak calmly and firmly, and back away slowly
   C. Make direct eye contact
   D. Try to touch the bear to show affection

5. What should you carry in areas where bears might be present?

   A. Bear repellent
   B. Food to feed the bears
   C. Loud music player
   D. Brightly colored clothing

6. What should you avoid doing if you accidentally approach a bee's nest?

   A. Make loud noises and swat at the bees
   B. Slowly perform a dance
   C. Cover your face and head with your hands or clothes
   D. Yell loudly to scare them away

7. What is the primary role of bees in nature?

   A. Producing honey for humans
   B. Pollinating plants
   C. Providing entertainment for children
   D. Controlling insect populations

8. How should you handle a venomous spider if necessary?

    A. Try to touch it with your bare hands
    B. Wear thick gloves or use a container to avoid contact
    C. Squash it with your foot
    D. Try to make it angry to see its venom in action

9. What should you do immediately after getting stung by a bee?

    A. Apply pressure around the sting area
    B. Leave the stinger in the skin
    C. Squeeze the sting area to get more venom
    D. Remove the stinger and wash the area with soap and water

10. What is a crucial step in preventing insect stings and bites?

    A. Wearing long sleeves and insect repellent
    B. Encouraging insects to bite you for fun
    C. Leaving food out in the open
    D. Ignoring insect repellent

Animal Dangers Maze

Embark on the Animal Dangers Maze Adventure! Guide your way through the twists and turns, avoiding perilous encounters with wild creatures. Can you navigate safely to the end without becoming prey?

RECAP OF KEY SURVIVAL TECHNIQUES LEARNED IN 10!

#1 Respect Nature - Always approach the wilderness with care and respect for the creatures that live there. Always remember, we humans are the visitors to their home!

#2 Stay Calm - In moments of danger or uncertainty, remain calm and think clearly (or try to!). Panicking can lead to poor decision-making. You've got to be a superhero to survive all of this! We know that you are. You've made it this far in the book, after all.

#3 Prepare Properly - Carry a backpack of all crucial equipment. Whether it's tents, shelters, water, food, drink, insect repellent, first aid kits, or bear spray, always prepare properly. Be ready for any situation that may arise.

#4 Handle Adverse Weather – remember all the tips for hurricane, tornado, and food survival? Of course you do! You can handle adverse weather like a pro, now. Treat powerful weather as a force: know that weather is strong and mighty. You can't fight it; you've got to appreciate and handle it.

#5 Animal Encounters - If you come across a snake, give it space and slowly back away. Don't touch or handle a wild snake, and always watch your step when in snake-prone areas. And bear aware (ha!). In regions where bears live, remain calm if you see one. Avoid running and make yourself appear larger by waving your arms. Carry bear spray just in case!

#6 Bee Cautious with Bees and Spiders - If you find a bee's nest, move away and avoid swatting at bees. Cover your face and head to avoid the most painful places where you might get stung. Learn to spot venomous spiders and steer clear.

#7 Sting and Bite First Aid - Know how to treat insect stings and bites. Remove stingers gently, clean the area, and apply cold compresses to reduce swelling.

#8 Keep Learning and Adapting – Wherever you are, and whatever you're doing, you'll be learning and improving. Whether you're in a submerging car or you're in the very remotest parts of the continent, you can always do your best. Continuously educate yourself about survival skills and wildlife behavior. Adapt your strategies based on new knowledge and experiences. Every time you enter new situations, you'll be bringing a wealth of knowledge with you.

#9 Be Street Smart – whether you are, you'll meet new people along the way. Remember to respect other people's places and cultures. Be open to learning about new ways of life. Look out! Look up! And always trust your instincts. If something feels strange or untoward, find a way to get out. Your instincts are usually right for keeping you safe. Listen to that inner voice of yours.

#10 Embrace Your Adventures - Above all, embrace your adventures! Enjoy exploring the great outdoors and this wonderful world. There is so much beauty and fun out there. It's waiting for you, brave explorer!

Here's the big question: are you ready?

We hope that you'll come back to this guide again and again. Treat it as your trusty companion. We want you to be fully equipped with our awesome survival guide.

The wilderness is not just a place of challenges; it's an empire of wonder and discovery! With every step, every creature, and every obstacle we overcome, we deepen our connection to nature and unlock the secrets of human survival.

It's in our nature to survive.

Can you focus on this? Can you push yourself to a limit?

Whether you're someone who wants to camp out under the stars, or simply create imaginary adventures in your backyard, let the spirit of adventure guide you. Let your brand-new knowledge be your compass (as well as your actual compass, don't forget!)

Be courageous. Be willing. Be open. There will be no stopping you.

As we close this book, you might be thinking… But I'm a kid. I can't go anywhere right now.

But one day you will. One day you can. One day, you'll be that grown-up adult planning to explore the world and be a globetrotter. Also, you never know when you'll need your survival skills: it might be a perfectly ordinary day when you need to administer CPR or save someone's life. You might still be 'a kid' when this situation arises.

We don't know what tomorrow holds.

So, go forth and embrace the future that awaits you. Prepare for wild wonder. Keep being you. Stay curious, and stay wild!

Happy adventuring, you awesome human!

Bonus Section

HOW TO SURVIVE A ZOMBIE APOCALYPSE!

Outstretch your arms in front of you, wince your eyes, and start mumbling… you must be a zombie! Right?

Wrong! Zombies aren't just mumbling sleepwalkers, they're supposedly hungry, dead folk looking to infect others. Gross? Or fun and fantastical? You decide!

Essentially, zombies are fantasy figures: they are reanimated corpses, which means they've come back to life after kicking the bucket (dying). And when a zombie re-emerges into the world, they're not happy about it. In fact, zombies tend to be synonymous with grumpy, green things.

Some people like to think that zombies want brains. Not brains to think, but brain to EAT! With that in mind, let's close our guidebook (if a zombie hasn't eaten it) by preparing you with how to survive a zombie apocalypse! Let's imagine an alternate universe, where for some crazy reason, an army of loose and wild zombies enter Earth trying to take over!

Brains, brains, yummy BRAINS… they're hungrily sourcing as many humans by the bulk. It's apocalyptic (end of the world). What should you do?

Secure Shelter! Find a location with limited doors or windows to keep zombies out. Keep your eyes peeled on any accessible points: prepare for what you're going to do if the zombies try to get inside! Hide. Duck down. Stick with family and friends. Form an army, perhaps. Prepare to stand up for all of humankind!

But don't forget your supplies. Stockpile food, water, and medical supplies. You'll need tools for defence and survival as you stay in your hideout. It could be the end of the world, after all. You're hardly going to want to run to the supermarket when the zombies are out! That's if the supermarket hasn't been overtaken by zombies already…

Keep tabs on the situation via radio, the internet (if available), or rely on messages from other survivors. The zombies might make you feel alone and detached from humanity, but staying connected to other humans might mean that you defeat the baddies and win!

If you must venture out of your hiding spot, travel quietly and cautiously, avoiding areas with high zombie presence. Do you have binoculars? Use them. Do you have a good instinct? Follow it.

Avoid loud sounds whenever possible. Don't draw attention to yourself. These zombies want to find you!

Be resourceful in the same way that you have learned before. Build a fire. Purify water. Protect yourself and stay within your shelter.

How will you defeat the zombies? That we can't say…

Perhaps you need to build a zombie contraption?

Perhaps you need a big hole that the zombies will all fall into?

Perhaps you need a giant fishing net to catch loose zombies?

Whatever you do, good luck in the zombie apocalypse.

We hope you SURVIVE!

Zombie Apocalypse Maze

Survive the Zombie Apocalypse Maze! Assist the hungry zombie in navigating through obstacles to reach the brains. Can you help him satisfy his hunger without getting bitten?

TRIVIA ANSWERS

Trivia #1:

1. B
2. A
3. C
4. C
5. A
6. C
7. B
8. C
9. C
10. D

Trivia #2:

1. B
2. B
3. C
4. D
5. D
6. A
7. B
8. A
9. B
10. D

Triva #3:

1. C
2. C
3. D
4. B

5. C
6. A
7. C
8. D
9. A
10. D

Trivia #4:

1. B
2. A
3. D
4. B
5. B
6. D
7. B
8. C
9. C
10. A

Trivia #5:

1. C
2. C
3. D
4. B
5. C
6. D
7. D
8. C
9. A
10. C

Trivia #6

1. C
2. A
3. A
4. B
5. A
6. C
7. B
8. B
9. D
10. A

First Aid & Emergency Care Crossword Puzzle Answers

Across:
- 1. SCENE
- 2. FILTER
- 3. SIGNAL
- 4. COMPRESSIONS
- 5. BANDAGE
- 6. CPR

Down:
- 1. MORSE
- 2. EMERGENCY
- 3. BREATH
- 4. CHOKING
- 5. FIRSTAID
- 6. WATER
- 7. RESCUE

Human Hazards Crossword Puzzle Answers

Wilderness Survival Word Search Puzzle Answers

Surviving Natural Disasters Word Search Puzzle Answers

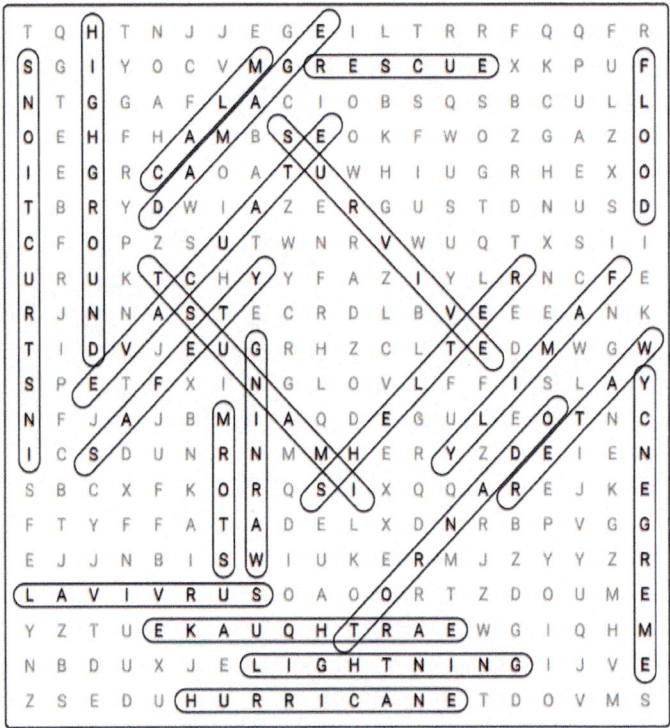

Printed in Great Britain
by Amazon

47402947R10099